The Plant Lover's
BACKYARD
FOREST GARDEN

Pippa Chapman

Permanent Publications

Published by
Permanent Publications
Hyden House Ltd
13 Clovelly Road
Portsmouth
PO4 8DL
United Kingdom
Tel: 01730 776 585
          International: +44 (0)1730 776 585
Email: enquiries@permaculture.co.uk
Web: www.permanentpublications.co.uk

Distributed in North America by
Chelsea Green Publishing Company, PO Box 428, White River Junction, VT 05001, USA
www.chelseagreen.com

Designed by Two Plus George Limited, info@twoplusgeorge.co.uk

Cover illustration by Stu McLellan, www.stumclellan.co.uk

Printed in the UK by Bell & Bain, Thornliebank, Glasgow

All paper from FSC certified mixed sources

The Forest Stewardship Council (FSC) is a non-profit international organisation
established to promote the responsible management of the world's forests.
Products carrying the FSC label are independently certified to assure consumers
that they come from forests that are managed to meet the social, economic and
ecological needs of present and future generations.

British Library Cataloguing-in-Publication Data
A catalogue record for this book is available from the British Library

ISBN 978 1 85623 287 6

Praise for the Book

As a bug and fresh food lover with a very small garden space, I was intrigued to find how useful and transformational this book was. Forests in my 10x10? Impossible! But it is the art (often literally) of the possible that the author, Pippa Chapman, shares here so well and the first pictures – there are many glorious photos – of 2x2m plots are utterly delightful, drawing you into the rest of an incredibly instructive book, full of ideas of how to grow with a 'multilayered' and diverse forest approach to bring flowers, food and life into your garden or plot. I've already got new plans for my wee space and it is hard to imagine anyone not thinking afresh after reading this, using all the tools and stages outlined so accessibly and compellingly here, to maximise the multiple products you can get – Pippa outlines seven at least, from food to fun.

Vicki Hird

Head of the Sustainable Farming Campaign for Sustain

If you dream of planting a forest garden but lack the space and know-how, this is the book for you. Pippa uses her vast practical knowledge of forest gardening and permaculture to show you how to create a garden that is both productive and beautiful. From planning to harvest, Pippa explains how to pack in the produce while also working with nature to produce a low maintenance haven for you, your family, and the wildlife that will become part of it.

Steve Ott

editor of *Kitchen Garden* magazine

A beautifully clear guide to using the principles of forest gardening on a garden scale that perfectly balances the practical and inspirational with Pippa's personal experience.

Mark Diacono

food writer, grower, photographer and cook

An inspiring and informative guide perfect for the aspiring food forest gardener. Pippa's expert advice speaks to both those who are just starting their permaculture journey as well as more experienced growers. She also shows that you don't need a large garden to create a beautiful and productive edible landscape.

Tanya Anderson

author, blogger and YouTube creator at Lovely Greens

This beautifully illustrated book is full of practical wisdom, but is never prescriptive, and there is plenty of emphasis on how the principles of forest garden design can be tweaked and adapted to suit your own needs and circumstances.

Graham Burnett

permaculture teacher and author of *The Vegan Book of Permaculture*

Acknowledgements

A huge thank you to my family who had total faith I could write this book even when I didn't. A special thanks to Chris Hardy without whom this book would never have been finished.

Contents

Foreword

I first met Pippa (and Andrew) when I organised an RHS Garden Bridgewater team day out to their garden and plant nursery in May 2019. As a team of horticulturists working on the early stages of a project, with only hard landscaping for company, we craved lush and abundant greenery. We certainly got that at Pippa's place, as well as delicious home-made cakes and coffee. The ingenuity of plants in the 'backyard' impressed us all – from pumpkins climbing up the washing line to perennial kale grown as a tree. As we toured around the wider garden, a combination that made a big impression on me was the gooseberries happily naturalising under the shade of a birch copse. They were the healthiest gooseberries I have ever seen! Not a sawfly or mildewed leaf in sight. A definite example of understanding what one plant needs (gooseberries and dappled shade), looking to other plants (birch) to help satisfy this need, and so creating a new mutually beneficial relationship between the two. The thorny gooseberries in turn protect the base of the birch from deer and rabbits.

When I started my gardening career over 20 years ago, edible horticulture was very much on the fringes. Permaculture and forest gardening were unquestionably niche – subversive almost! You most definitely would not have found them on the horticultural curriculum. Having trained in a botanic garden, many of the concepts and principles of permaculture I learnt years later, though logical to me, definitely upended much of what I had studied. Thankfully things have changed and curricula are now broader, with a clear ecological slant and often with an element of environmental sociology. Indeed forest gardens and their ability to connect people, plants and place have become a valuable tool in community engagement, education and environmentalism. The inclusion of one, designed by Harris Bugg Studio, in the newly opened RHS Garden Bridgewater indicates just how ubiquitous they have become.

Forest gardens are perhaps the oldest form of gardening. Our prehistoric ancestors would have relied on the forest for survival – learning which plants were good for food, medicine or shelter. Plants that were not useful were removed and those that were, were nurtured and protected. Eventually plants gathered elsewhere were incorporated, as was livestock. These 'gardens' created through observation and experimentation were not for just growing food, they became fundamental to the continued existence of their creators.

Indeed scaled up forest gardens, agroforestry systems as they are known, are still common in the tropics for growing familiar crops such as coffee and bananas. In the UK, small-scale market gardeners also realise the ecological and cropping potential of forest gardens – which are often planted in a linear fashion (termed an 'alley' or linear forest garden or linear polyculture) to allow vegetable beds or livestock grazing in between rows.

We look to forests for escape, for solace from everyday life. Green is good for you! Every time we walk through mixed woodland, we experience a forest garden in its wild form. Forest gardening is nature mimicry at its finest. It is about observing the relationships between plants, animals and fungi in woodland, and using those principles to recreate that jigsaw of interactions in your own space, but with plants that are of use to you.

As a dyed-in-the-wool kitchen gardener, I am always interested in shoehorning something edible into any available space. Forest gardens go beyond 'traditional' methods of food growing, and almost become an immersive experience, giving you the freedom to experiment and broadening the meaning of what makes a garden productive. You could say that forest gardening is the fusion of foraging and gardening.

As well as being a trained horticulturist and nurserywoman, Pippa is an experienced permaculture practitioner. The wonder of this book is that it is based on extensive experience. Much knowledge and effortless expertise are packed into it, but it is written in an extremely accessible way. It is practical but not prescriptive, and clearly explains the principles and philosophy behind forest gardening. It empowers both the novice and seasoned gardener. Pippa enables you to turn the limitations of your space (size, aspect, soil), or of you (time, experience), into opportunities – she has a useful plant or combination for any niche. Observation is at the very heart of a forest garden and Pippa makes clear that small tweaks can have a significant impact on you and your garden.

Forest gardening encourages us to reflect on the role we have to play in our own gardens and how we can effect change, no matter how small. There is an inherent contradiction in gardening – that it is intrinsically beneficial to our environment. It frequently is the opposite – the use of peat, monocultural food production and chemical pest and disease control, to name but a few. However I have hope that the popularity of forest gardening marks a shift towards more ethical gardening, an unlearning of sorts, a reconnection with environmental and human wellbeing very much at its heart.

Dr Sylvia Travers
No-dig kitchen and market gardener
with a PhD in pomology and plant science

Introduction

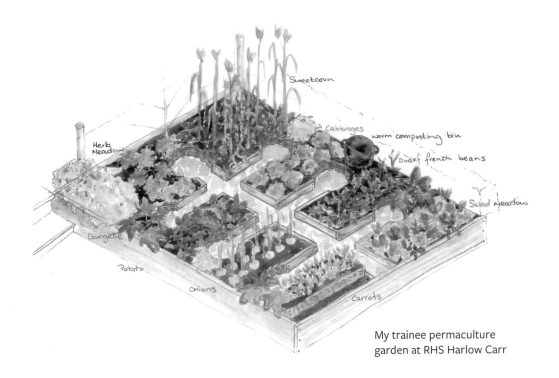

My trainee permaculture
garden at RHS Harlow Carr

In 2007 I made an odd career move to go from head gardener on a large private estate to trainee with the RHS. Sometimes a thirst for knowledge overrules any sensible career progression plans. It proved to be one of the best decisions I ever made for it was here that I first came across the concept of forest gardens. Plans were in place for an acre of forest garden at Harlow Carr in North Yorkshire, and I couldn't wait to get involved. Sadly the forest garden was never planted, but my forest gardening journey had started. It had sparked my curiosity to find out more about this fascinating way of growing food. This was the beginning of my permaculture journey. During my year-long apprenticeship, I gained a huge wealth of knowledge about gardening and alongside this I began looking into permaculture and more eco-friendly ways to garden. I visited as many permaculture gardens as I could until, in 2010, I decided to create my own, with grand plans to plant up a whole acre on my parents' land. This meant a move to their smallholding in West Yorkshire. In quite quick succession I started a sustainable gardening business with my now husband, Andrew, and started a family. Frustratingly having made the move to the smallholding, mobility problems during and after pregnancy, plus the addition of a baby meant my gardening was mostly confined to our yard, a relatively small and uninspiring space of paving and untidy grass.

During my time at Harlow Carr, I designed and planted up a permaculture plot. I had an epiphany,

A 'meadow' polyculture of annual salads and vegetables

what I felt to be a genius idea of growing lots of crops mixed together rather than in rows. I named this 'vegetable and herb meadows'. I had experimented, pretty unsuccessfully, on the training plots at Harlow Carr. Now faced with bare soil again I felt inspired to continue with these experiments. The first trials were mostly a mix of annual herbs, flowers, salad leaves and vegetables, which looked lovely in summer and autumn but not great through the winter. What I was really craving was more structure, colour and flowers. Over time I added in the odd perennial flowering plant, then a small apple tree and a couple of pears relocated from Andrew's nan's garden, which we trained against the wall. Then one day whilst doing the washing up I looked out of the window with the sudden realisation that I had created a forest garden, small though it was, abundant in a huge diversity of food and teeming with wildlife.

In slow incremental steps, I had transformed my idea of a vegetable and herb meadow by adding height in the form of small fruit trees, perennial kale and climbers. It looked just like a miniature woodland but everything was edible or useful to me in some way. This way of growing really excites me as it fulfils both my love of growing food, but also my desire to grow beautiful gardens which are a pleasure to spend time in. The yard is the view from most rooms in the house so it has to look appealing; it is also the most accessible location in which to grow food so it makes perfect sense to do both in the same space.

This book is not typical of most forest garden books. It concentrates on small-scale spaces which

A mini forest garden bed 2 x 2m with perennial kale as the canopy layer

The yard forest garden in September

An arch for supporting peas and nasturtiums doubles as a play area in our small yard. Photo: Neil Chapman

Our first attempts at polycultures in the yard

are the reality of what is available for the majority of people. For most, owning an acre or two and creating a forest garden is an impossible dream, limited by time, money, availability or other life commitments. So here's my proposition: why not work with what you already have? Don't view the space as a limitation, rather as a challenge to your imagination. Whether you have an average or small front or back garden or yard, or you want to create a forest garden patch in a small part of a larger garden, this book will guide you through a step-by-step process with practical hints, tips and inspiration along your forest garden adventure. Even if all you can squeeze in is a large planter or container, this book will offer some solutions to grow a beautiful and productive micro garden. So turn the page and get started on your forest garden journey.

Flowers, fruit, herbs and vegetables creating a beautiful forest garden border

A small-scale multi-layered edible polyculture mimicking a forest ecosystem

CHAPTER 1

What is Forest Gardening?

The term refers to how we can grow food in a multi-layered way, learning from a forest ecosystem. You are not gardening in a forest, you are gardening by observing how a forest functions, mimicking its structure and ecosystems. By looking at how a forest grows we can learn a lot about how plants can create a multi-layered system where plants successfully coexist. We can mimic that natural system in our own gardens. This is very different to traditional vegetable gardens, which work against nature to keep bare soil weed-free between plants, whilst separating individual species. By working with nature we can create low maintenance and productive gardens that are a haven for wildlife and ourselves.

The most diverse growth phase of a forest is when it is a young woodland. At this point it will have the largest range of different plants due to some areas still receiving light whilst also having shady places, providing a wide range of growing conditions. There is also the productive edge where woodland meets grassland. Here there is still enough light reaching the ground between the trees to allow shrubs and other groundcover plants to thrive. In most mature forests in the British temperate climate, the canopy has formed a dense barrier to catch all available sunlight, little light reaches the forest floor and only shade-loving plants can survive. By growing like a forest, rather than in an actual forest, and learning from nature, we can make the most of beneficial relationships while producing food to eat. This chapter explores some of these benefits and how you can apply them in your own small space.

Benefits of forest gardening
Monoculture vs polyculture

A monoculture is when only one type of plant is grown in an area of land, such as a field of wheat or an apple orchard. This uses only one layer of available vertical space. Any pest or disease which finds its way to one plant could then easily spread to the rest of the crop. If the weather one year is too wet to harvest the wheat, or a late frost ruins the apple blossom, the whole crop is ruined.

A polyculture is where different plants are grown together, often with plants growing at varying heights, such as in forest gardening. Crops are chosen to complement each other so one does not outcompete the other. This way if pests, disease or weather conditions cause one crop to give a poor yield, you still have the harvest from the others. Pests find it more difficult to find plants they predate on when grown in a mixed setting so tend not to spread as far, which creates a more resilient growing environment, therefore a more resilient ecosystem. There are also many

▶ Edible hawthorn with kale, rhubarb and lemon balm amongst others growing in one corner of the lawn at Ecology Building Society

▼ A very colourful polyculture of annual vegetables, salad and perennial herbs

◄ Edible and ornamental plants growing together in flower borders and vertically as a green wall

► A quite wild mini forest garden; the groundcover comfrey is alive with bees, attracting pollinators at the same time the apple is flowering

opportunities for creating beneficial relationships and bigger yields can be obtained as you are using the vertical space. If you design a really successful polyculture, the combination of plants can create a synergistic effect with the garden producing more than the sum of its parts.

Diversity of crops gives resilience. It seems our climate is destined to become more and more unpredictable in the future. This means some years may bake the garden dry, other years it may be saturated, and if we are really unlucky we have both extremes in the same year. If we have a large diversity of crops, some will do well in wet years, and others when it's dry. By using polycultures we should always get a yield.

Forest garden polycultures provide habitat for wildlife. There are few monocultures that are great

habitats for wildlife. The diversity of wildlife exploded in our yard once we got rid of the grass and planted it up, especially after the addition of shrubs and small trees. In our tiny yard we have robins, blue tits and a blackbird who nest every year. I have even had a young kestrel come to visit. We have also seen a huge range of insects, luckily mostly beneficial.

There are so many yields from a forest garden in addition to food; this is explained in more detail later in the chapter.

Perennial plantings such as trees, shrubs and herbaceous perennials build soils rather than deplete them; this will be discussed in more detail in Chapter 7. Many annual crops, especially those grown in containers, require a lot of fresh compost each year.

By practising no-till gardening, the soil food web begins to flourish. Mulching (spreading organic matter on top of the soils) each year means constantly adding to the soil and feeding soil life.

The garden can create its own fertility. Clever use of nitrogen fixing and dynamic accumulator plants (see Chapter 4) can increase the fertility of your garden rather than deplete it. Synthetic fertilisers are damaging to soil life and can leave plants more prone to attack from pests and disease, just as with us if we ate a poor diet of highly processed food. Designing a self-sustaining cycle of fertility means your garden will be very resilient, have low inputs and work more in tune with nature.

Limitations of forest gardening

I may be biassed but I can think of very few limitations to this way of growing. It can take longer to get a crop because many plants, such as the shrubs and fruit trees, may not crop well until year two or three, but once they are established they can outyield mono-crop beds. It is cheap to buy a few packets of seeds and grow some annual vegetables when compared with the bigger investment of perennials. However the perennials will come back each year and once they have reached a decent size, cuttings or divisions can be swapped or bartered for more plants.

Crops are spread out, especially in larger forest gardens, so harvesting can be more time consuming than if each crop was handily grown in the same row or block. Harvesting is a joy to me; I love to potter through the garden picking tiny alpine strawberries or taking a few kale leaves from the few plants dotted around, so if we look at the problem being the solution, it gives us an excuse to spend a little extra time in our wonderful patch of wilderness. A big difference with a forest garden is it tends not to be as neat as more traditional gardens. To this I would say there is a definite need to be a more relaxed gardener; by being neat you are removing vital habitat.

Harvesting kale for dinner as I do some
pruning and weeding

Yields from a forest garden

We are only limited by our imaginations (and space) so it is valuable to consider that not all yields of a forest garden are edible. Forest gardens are a poly-culture of multi-purpose plants. These have been handily named the seven Fs.

Food
Fuel
Fibre
Fodder
Fertiliser
'Ph'armaceutical
Fun

Pumpkins can be grown up a structure to give
a high yield without taking up much space

▲ Willow can be grown as a coppiced hedge

▶ Coppiced willow can be used to make obelisks and fencing

⏩ Leave sunflower heads for the birds to forage from

Food – Well this is the most obvious yield in a forest garden.

Fuel – In a small space this doesn't apply so easily as you are unlikely to plan firewood as a main crop if you only have a few square metres. (Though you may decide to save up a few small twigs and dried leaves which might just boil enough water to enjoy a tea from a Kelly Kettle.)

Fibre – Many plants can be processed for their fibres to create twine or textiles. I like to plant a *Phormium* (New Zealand flax) where there is space. It is very satisfying and easy to peel off thin strips of the leaves to tie in peas or other climbers. It is surprisingly strong and lasts a whole season. A very strong twine can be made from nettles and other plants with long fibres by bashing the stem to separate the fibres, drying them, then twisting them in a way that the fibres hold tightly together. It is very time consuming but a lovely meditative task to undertake on a rainy day, although it takes so long it feels too precious to use to tie up peas. Willow is another material you can grow to weave and build structures.

Fodder – This is food for animals. If you are growing in a small space it is unlikely you are going to be harvesting armfulls of leafy branches to feed to sheep and goats. You may however have smaller pets who may like to nibble dandelion, sunflower seeds or other leafy crops, so this may be a consideration when deciding what to grow. It's great to find other yields you hadn't considered before. I have even had a request for my apple prunings as it is a wood that is safe for hamster chews.

I like to think of the fodder for wildlife. Flowering plants provide pollen and nectar. Sometimes just changing your garden practices can provide another yield. Try leaving seed heads to overwinter as a food source for birds and small mammals, and don't strip every single berry from fruit bushes; leave a few as a reward to the wildlife for keeping all those pests in check.

Fertiliser – I will go into more detail later but an important part of a forest garden system is to provide at least some of its own fertiliser. In nature there is no one to feed the plants. The natural cycle of things growing, dying, decaying on the surface and returning to the earth keeps everything fed. Where animals are eating some of the crop, they return those nutrients through faeces and eventually dying and returning to the soil. This is not possible on a small scale in our own food forests so we need to grow plants that can do some of this by bringing nutrients up from deep down in the ground or by fixing nitrogen from the air.

Pharmaceutical – Herbs and medicinal plants can be grown within the polyculture. I love the idea of growing my own first aid kit just on my doorstep. Herbs are not just for cooking; I enjoy harvesting leaves and flowers from the garden and creating my own herbal tea blends. I make a few separate teapots with individual herbs or flowers, then pour different combinations into a cup and make notes of those I like. Once the herbs and flowers are dried I combine them to use throughout the year.

There are so many pharmaceutical uses for plants, it's well worth doing a bit of research, especially if you have any specific ailments. Team up with friends and neighbours if space is really limited and form a 'first aid kit' of medicinal plants spread throughout many gardens.

Fun – Our enjoyment of the space, and the enjoyment of the process of gardening are often forgotten when thinking of yields, even more so when space is limited and the food growing and socialising happens in the same space.

▲ Lemon balm is said to help reduce stress and anxiety and provide relief from insomnia and indigestion

▶ I love to weave with willow so have included structures where I can. This living willow archway needs a bit of additional weaving and pruning in summer to stop it taking over, a lovely way to spend a sunny afternoon

This pear 'Durondeau' is lovely and crisp

Snacking on wild strawberries

The pattern of a forest garden

The ecology of a young woodland has been handily broken down into seven layers. Each layer is at a different level so they are not competing for growing space. The ideal is that your forest garden will incorporate plants from each layer to maximise use of the vertical space within your garden. In reality there is no strict rule that says if yours only has four or five layers you cannot call it a forest garden. It is an aspiration, and especially on a smaller scale, all seven layers can be difficult to achieve.

The seven layers of a forest garden: Canopy, lower tree, shrub, herbaceous, groundcover, rhizosphere and climbing

Seven layers of a forest garden

Examples of each layer will be discussed in Chapter 3.

1 Canopy layer

These are the tallest trees such as nut trees or large fruit trees. In small gardens this layer is usually absent as many gardens wouldn't manage to accommodate even one large tree, never mind allow any light to reach the floor for the other layers.

2 Lower tree layer

Dwarf fruit and nut trees, usually under 3m in height.

3 Shrub layer

These are usually currant bushes or other berries.

4 Herbaceous layer

These are the plants that will grow each year but die right back to ground level in the winter, unless they are evergreen. They are distinguished from the shrubs by the absence of a permanent branching structure.

Dahlia tubers can be roasted and eaten like potatoes

5 Groundcover layer

Plants that hug the ground; these are usually spreading plants that grow along the soil surface and cover the bare ground.

6 Rhizosphere

Many think of the soil surface as the lowest layer, however many plants have edible roots. Several of our staple crops grow in the rhizosphere, such as carrots and potatoes.

7 Climbing plants

Plants in this group climb upwards to make the most of all the available vertical space by climbing through all the other layers.

Perennial plants are those that grow for more than two years. Forest gardens are mostly made up of perennial plants such as fruit and nut trees, fruiting bushes, herbs and perennial vegetables. This makes them very resilient as a growing system as they will come back each year with the minimum of effort. With an annual vegetable garden, you need to sow seed each year, at just the right time to get a crop. This perennial aspect has been a very valuable trait on many occasions such as when the children were small and I had no time for gardening or when I once had the flu and was in bed from January until March and missed sowing many annual crops. The perennial plants still sprung up from the earth regardless and gave a yield.

How can the seven layers be applied on a small garden scale?

Above I have described the ideal structure of a forest garden. When scaling this down we need to make adaptations. It helps to realise that even in natural woodlands and forests, layers will be missing. Not all woodland has climbers; dense woodland such as beech often has very little undergrowth as the trees catch all the available light and fallen leaves decompose slowly.

Many layers can be achieved
even in a small space

1. The canopy layer

This is the most obvious problem in a small space. This layer usually consists of very large nut, fruit and even timber trees. If you have an existing tree, it can serve as the canopy layer, although it may be worth considering crown lifting it (removing the lower branches) where appropriate to allow more light in. If not, then miss out this layer.

2. Lower tree layer

Fruit trees such as apple, pear, plum and cherry and small nuts, such as hazel, usually make up the lower canopy layer. Some trees have a more upright, columnar growth habit such as crab apple 'Maypole'; this makes the most of the vertical space where growing room is limited. You may feel you don't even have space for one of these but you can buy fruit on a variety of rootstocks. The role of a rootstock is to control the vigour (size) of the tree and in some cases improve disease resistance. A named variety of fruit is grafted onto a rootstock and forms a union, with the tree continuing to grow as one. Many different varieties can be grown as large, medium or small trees, enabling a wide range of fruit to be grown in small gardens and even large pots. You can also wall train most fruit to use even less space.

If you are looking to buy dwarf fruit it is best to find a good local nursery that can advise of varieties suitable for your area. See page 117 for full details on dwarf rootstocks.

These plants can be kept to a suitable size with pruning and training which will be discussed in more detail later in the book. If space is really limited, fruit can be trained against a wall or even as a fence so you can use the vertical space without limiting what you can grow beneath it.

▲ Training fruit against a wall allows more plants in a small space. Photo: Neil Chapman

◄ Espaliered pear in a traditional kitchen garden. What a shame the space underneath is wasted.

Eleagnus umbellata has small but beautifully scented flowers in spring

Kale 'Panache' is a low-growing smothering shrub that is happy in part shade

3. Shrub layer

Currants and other fruiting bushes usually make up the shrub layer although there are plants with other uses such as nitrogen fixing plants like *Eleagnus umbellata* (autumn olive) or plants for weaving such as willow (*Salix*) or *Cornus* (dogwoods). In a small space, you need to decide your priorities for the function of the plants. Perhaps your friend has a field of currants you can forage from, or your neighbour is forever filling your cupboards with more jam than you can eat and really you would love to weave with willow you have grown yourself. I have squeezed a few ornamental shrubs into my yard such as hydrangea and roses, as it is my main area for sitting so it needs to look great too.

As with larger fruit trees, some currants such as red, white and pink currants and gooseberries can be trained against a wall. Look out for varieties that are described as fastigiate (tall and slim) or compact that can grow in a small space. Jostaberries are fantastic but mine is roughly 3m diameter and pruning just seems to make it put on even more vigorous growth the following year.

I would include perennial kale in the shrub layer too due to its size and evergreen nature. My favourite variety 'Taunton Deane' has a very sprawling habit and can become huge, as it grows up then flops over, usually onto other plants if I am not paying attention. I have one in the yard which I have trained as a 'tree' by staking it up and removing the lower branches as it grows, making it the canopy layer in my yard forest garden. I just love kale.

4. Herbaceous layer

This layer has many possibilities even in the smallest of spaces. It includes many herbs, perennial salad plants and vegetables. Most of this layer would happily grow in a pot where space and soil are really limited. It is almost harder to decide what to grow in this layer as there is so much choice. On the plus side, it's easier to make changes and tweaks to this layer than to dig up and move a tree or shrub, meaning experimentation is easier. I will describe later how to put together your carefully thought through design but often I just throw things in the ground and see what happens – it has taken years to know what will work. The main considerations in this layer are whether your plants are edible, ornamental or one of the other Fs, and obviously size and vigour. If you really want to include something that is vigorous, such as comfrey 'Bocking 14', you just need to keep an eye out so that it doesn't swamp out other plants.

Annual salads mixed with other herbs and flowers. It looks beautiful and provides plenty of crops for the kitchen.

5. Groundcover

In nature there is rarely bare soil, unless there has been fire, avalanche or some other disaster to remove vegetation. If we remove the 'weeds' from a garden, we create a lovely seedbed for new 'weeds' to germinate and 'heal' the wound. Most garden soil has seed lying dormant under the surface. When we dig, we bring these to the surface where conditions are right for germination. The best way to prevent, or at least hugely reduce, the need for weeding is to cover all soil with things we want to grow. Ground-cover plants do this job brilliantly. They spread out along the soil surface, filling in all the gaps left by other plants. Wild strawberries and *Ajuga* (bugle) are amongst my favourites. The former I enjoy more than the usual cultivated varieties and the latter is wonderful for bees, and the glossy purple leaves are a great backdrop for other plants.

Wild strawberry, *Sedum* and *Ajuga* make a very effective ground cover to prevent weed seeds from germinating

6. Rhizosphere

When space is at a premium it pays to prioritise the value you get from each crop. Organic carrots and potatoes are relatively easy to get hold of these days so does it make sense to grow them amongst plants whose roots you will destroy when harvesting? There are some smaller and more special root crops such as oca or Chinese artichokes that would suit smaller gardens. Not exactly a staple crop but something a bit unusual to add diversity to your diet.

Digging can disturb the root systems of surrounding plants and will damage soil life in the immediate area so you may decide not to include root crops; that's fine, you are still practising forest gardening. All your plants will be using the rhizosphere for root growth and access to nutrients and water, keeping the soil life healthy.

Oca freshly dug up from the forest garden

7. Climbing plants

Climbers are brilliant for small spaces. They grow upwards, using the valuable vertical space. They can hug walls and create huge plants whilst only using a very small amount of the ground/flower bed space or grow over arches and pergolas to create shady spaces allowing respite from the hot summer sun. With careful planning you can grow two or more climbers in the same space, further enhancing the diversity of your garden. I often add an archway or obelisk in my designs to increase the opportunities to add climbers. Small fruit trees will not tolerate the weight or competition from most climbing plants so whilst we may imagine an abundant small forest, trees hanging with lush vines, the reality is that dwarf trees have been created by reducing vigour and won't cope well with added stresses.

Hopefully the patterns described in this chapter will have given you an idea of how you can learn from the layers found in nature and apply them in your own small patch. My aim has been to encourage you to gain inspiration from nature but feel free to adapt the rules to suit your situation. Forest gardens can have multiple functions; take time to consider which yields and functions are your priority as this will inform the rest of the design when creating your own forest garden.

Shipping container eco office at Ecology Building Society reduces the carbon footprint of the business

CHAPTER 2

The Permaculture Design Process

What is permaculture?

It began as a concept developed by David Holgrem and Bill Mollison who abbreviated the words permanent and agriculture to create permaculture, describing the development of a self-sufficient, sustainable form of agriculture. As the movement has developed, the scope of permaculture has evolved to become more holistic, often described as creating a permanent culture rather than limited to food growing. It is underpinned by a set of ethics and principles that can help guide you towards a more sustainable way of living, starting to break down the concept of permaculture and steering us in the right direction. The design process itself is key to applying permaculture.

The three ethics

Earth care – Care of the earth underpins everything. When designing you must try to take into account how each element of your forest garden, from the planting, to irrigation to building materials, affects the planet and its delicate ecosystem. Can the creation of your forest garden have a regenerative effect on the earth rather than a negative impact?

People care – This can be on a personal level, a community level or a global level. Our forest garden may be kind to the planet but we aim to ensure people are not exploited during the creation of materials or plants and that we do not create negative relationships with our neighbours and wider community. How might we create beneficial human relationships with the creation of the forest garden? Could you help foster a culture of self-sufficiency in your neighbourhood? Can the garden help with our mental and physical health?

Fair share – We only have one earth. In the Global North we use much more than our fair share of resources. There are similar imbalances within our own communities. This ethic asks us to consider how these imbalances can be remedied. Could you donate some plants to a community project, perhaps after your garden is established and you have some cuttings or divisions to spare? Could you share surplus yields with local food banks, community cafes, family or friends?

◄ Plants ready for a plant swap at a local allotment

▲ Don't forget time and space to spend with friends and family. Photo: Neil Chapman

► We share fruit with our lovely friend Kate who then pays us back in the form of delicious jams

Gooseberry and Elderflower Butter 30.7.21

Seedlings of plants growing for our forest garden and our plant nursery

Principles

Permaculture principles help us to think in a new way whilst applying the three ethics. They are thinking tools aiding us to take a fresh perspective at how our designs can be low-carbon, eco-friendly and culturally beneficial for us and the wider community. There are several sets of principles developed by various perma-culture designers and practitioners. I tend to use David Holgrem's 12 principles, listed below, but there are others. They may seem a bit abstract but the more you use them the more helpful they become. I have included examples of how each could be applied to the design of a small-scale forest garden.

Obtain a yield

This one may seem obvious when talking about an edible garden, but consider all the other possible yields. Wildlife habitat, carbon capture, a source of seeds for a seed swap, socialising space, enjoyment and learning.

Design from pattern to detail

When I started my permaculture journey I kept thinking too literally of a visual pattern. A decade later I can honestly say that applying this principle has revolutionised my designing. In the design process the pattern is the bigger picture, which is broken down into smaller levels of detail, making things less overwhelming.

Many people struggle with achieving year-round interest in the garden. If you break the pattern of the year into smaller chunks, either months or seasons, you can begin to fill in the detail of the plants and ensure there is a balance between each category. Nature also has some wonderful visual patterns we can mimic in our gardens such as spirals and honeycombs.

Use small and slow solutions

Keep things simple, and manageable. Plant up a layer or small group of plants each year. Try to propagate some of your plants rather than buying them all. Start small and slow; this helps prevent that feeling of being too overwhelmed to make a start.

Herbs for drying

Willow cut from the forest garden and bundled ready for weaving bed edges

I took this photo in Filey and want to do something similar in my garden, inspired by the spiral shape of ammonites we find on the beach

▲ The oregano in the yard attracts pollinating insects when it is in flower but I cut it back once the flowers have finished so I get another flush of tender leaves

◀ Reusable Weck jars are fantastic for preserving our tomatoes

▶ 'Crown Prince' squash curing at room temperature in the hallway ready to be stored for use all winter and spring of the following year

Observe and interact

Good observation is vital to developing a successful forest garden. Does the kale 'Panache' keep wilting in full sun? Move it somewhere shady. Thyme keeps dying off as other plants swamp it out; lift it up in a pot where there is less competition. I don't spend enough time outdoors in the winter; could I add a firepit to entice me out? We can learn so much from observing and acting upon what we see. Keeping a diary can help.

Catch and store energy

We want to capture our gluts and store them for lean times. This may be in the form of a water butt, solar panels, composting or dehydrating and bottling foods. I capture my ideas in a notebook; sometimes I glue in scraps I have scribbled when I am out and about in case I forget them.

Apply self-regulation and accept feedback

Nature does this really well, humans not so well. Ask yourself what is going well and what is not, and be honest (don't forget to be kind to yourself; this is a positive step towards improvements, not a time for judgement). How can we improve, not just the forest garden but our relationship with the garden and the wider community? I love inviting others to spend time in my garden; all the positive comments remind me to appreciate the successes rather than dwelling on the failures.

Use and value renewable resources and services

Wherever possible I use pre-loved or locally grown materials. Take a holistic view of the garden implementation. Could you build raised beds and garden furniture from pallet wood or reclaimed timber? Garden lighting or pond pumps could be solar powered. Wooden plant labels look more attractive and can be made from garden prunings or foraged branches.

Produce no waste

Outputs from one element can become inputs for another element. The most basic example is composting garden waste and kitchen scraps to return nutrients and organic matter to the soil. Buying plants bare root (not in pots) eliminates plastic waste and junk. We flush valuable nutrients down the toilet everyday; urine is ideal for plant food (liquid gold!).

▲ This pallet provides vertical growing space for herbs and strawberries

◄ My father-in-law built this fantastic bench from pallets; he even included integrated tables at either side for work colleagues to use at lunch time

◄ Growing flowers and food crops together means we don't have to choose one over the other. We can choose plants that form beneficial relationships.

► Sedum kept self-seeding into this gravel from the green roof and was impossible to weed out so we decided to embrace it and plant it with alpines and create a gravel garden

◄ Mullein (*Verbascum*), sedum and *Verbena bonariensis* flourish in the gravel

Integrate rather than segregate

Can an element perform more than one function? Seating with storage built in for tools, a fruit tree for food and shade. It may also mean adding in elements for other members of the household and wider community, polycultures of both plants and people.

Use and value diversity

The most resilient systems have a lot of diversity. If one element fails, others are there to take over.

Use edges and value the marginal

Often the most productive area in a forest is its edges. This can be true of the edges between many aspects of life, such as work and home life. The edge between indoor and outdoor is often the most used; make the most of this valuable space.

Creatively use and respond to change

Whenever life throws me lemons, and there have been plenty, I like to reflect upon this principle. Can you find a silver lining and exploit it? In the garden, each season gives us another opportunity.

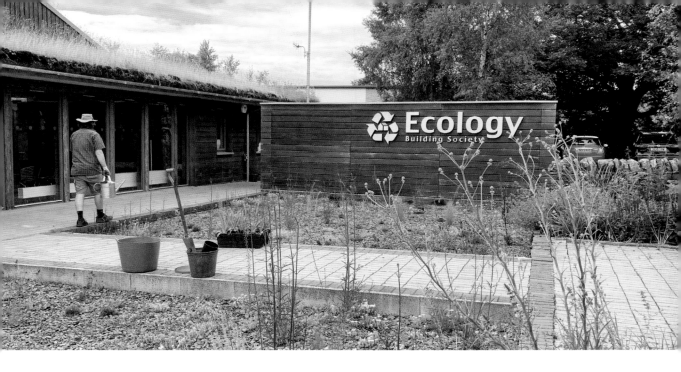

Permaculture gardening techniques and features

I have visited many permaculture gardens and forest gardens, some I loved and others that felt more like a tick list of permaculture garden features, sometimes used in inappropriate places. Good permaculture design is all about using appropriate technology or solutions rather than blindly copying something you read in a book or online. Here I introduce a few of these that you could incorporate into your designs if it is appropriate or needed.

Keyhole beds

These keyhole-shaped features allow easy access to all plants within a bed. With a narrow path and larger circle for easy turning around, they are much easier to use than balancing on stepping stones, although in many gardens stepping stones within beds are a very simple and effective way to harvest out-of-reach plants. You can use them singly or have multiple keyholes which can add to the aesthetics of the garden too. I have used cut dogwoods and willow for the circular section of the keyhole on raised beds where you can't use timber edging. If you want to construct the keyhole from timber you could simplify the circle to a hexagon or octagon. I have to say my woodworking skills don't stretch to accurately cutting so many angles, whereas I actively look for a good excuse for a bit of weaving. It doesn't need raised edges if that doesn't fit in with your design; you can simply demarcate the shape straight onto the ground.

Keyhole beds allow good access for harvesting and maintenance

Mandala garden

Mandala is Sanskrit for circle. These are circular-shaped gardens with paths and beds inside the circle making geometric patterns. They are usually associated with creating spiritual spaces.

Herb spiral

A herb spiral is roughly conical in shape, with the centre being highest and spiralling down to ground level. Not all herbs like the same conditions so by using a herb spiral, in theory, there is a sunny side, a shady side and the middle at the top will be better drained than the base of the spiral, providing a wide range of growing conditions. Nutrient levels are supposed to be higher at the outer parts of the spiral due to them washing down from the top of the spiral but I am not convinced this makes much difference. I think as a design feature they look great but feel the benefits of growing herbs this way have been exaggerated. If you have wet or boggy soil, it would be beneficial to grow on a mound to give plant roots more soil above the saturation level. I have seen many examples of trees planted successfully on mounds in wet soils; wouldn't it be lovely to have a forest garden spiral with the other layers spiralling downwards and outwards?

Sketching out ideas for mandala gardens

Hugel beds

If you have the opposite problem and you are on dry soil that struggles to hold onto moisture, you can practice hugelkultur, meaning hill or mound culture. The basic idea is to bury logs and branches under the soil to create a mound and plant into this. This has the multiple benefits of holding onto moisture as the decaying wood acts like a sponge; making water available to the plants during dry periods; building fertility as nutrients are slowly released as the wood decomposes; and increasing the surface area in which you can grow crops, meaning more plants in the same space. As with the herb spiral, many different microclimates can be created.

As the wood decomposes, it will feed the soil life creating soil conditions ideal for perennial and woodland plants such as fruit trees and bushes. If you have the space, a hugel bed could become an attractive garden feature, breaking up the space or masking an eyesore. If you are starting with a lawn, strip off the turf, dig a trench about a spit deep (the length of the blade of your spade), and fill the trench with logs, branches, leaves and any other organic material you can get hold of. Then cover with the removed turfs, placing them grass side down, and ideally covering with homemade compost or soil. You can then plant straight into this.

Compost is great for layering in your lasagne beds but you can build it with fresh materials and wait for it to compost in situ

Lasagne bed

As the name suggests, this technique requires the layering of organic materials to form a new planting bed. This is particularly useful if you have poor or sandy soil which loses moisture easily or lacks organic matter. It's also a great way to get started without having to disturb soil or clear weedy ground. The first step is to gather together lots of organic matter, ideally a good balance of green and brown matter. Green matter includes grass clippings, weeds, vegetable peelings etc., brown waste includes leaves, card, straw and other carbon rich materials.

To start the bed, squash down or cut down any weeds on the surface. Leave any cut weeds or grass in situ; this will simply rot down and add to the nutrients in the bed. Now cover the whole area with cardboard or three to four layers of newspaper. Make sure each piece has a good overlap to ensure there are no gaps. Once in place water well; this will help to kick-start the composting process. You can now begin alternating layers of green and brown materials. Once you have finished your layers, ideally achieving a total height of 50-60cm, top with card or straw to exclude light, then leave. If your materials are quite dry, it will help to water each layer as you build it. Dry materials will compost much more slowly.

A good time to start building your lasagne bed is the summer or autumn, before you want to plant it up. If you want to grow in it straight away, top the bed with around 10cm of topsoil or homemade compost to give seedlings something to grow in whilst the lower layers compost. If you are wanting to plant perennials it really is best to leave it a year to fully compost and settle. Even better, if you have an abundance of homemade compost or well-rotted manure, you can use that as the middle layer and plant straight into it. Once your bed is finished, you simply mulch each year with well-rotted compost, ramial woodchip (smaller pieces of chip, often from young branches, which are high in cambium and break down quicker) or other organic matter.

Zoning

When considering zoning on a permaculture site it usually refers to five zones, on a large scale. The area closest to the property, zone 1, is where you place the activities you do most often; this is where the most intensive gardening happens and is the area most often visited. Zone 2 might include chickens and other animals needing daily attention, fruit trees, elements you visit less often. Zone 3 might include pasture, larger fruit and nut trees, Zone 4 could include trees for timber and areas to forage. Finally Zone 5 is left unmanaged, for the benefit of wildlife.

The concept of designing for the most intensive activities to happen nearest to the house is still a useful one, even in a small garden. Take a single flower bed as an example. Herbs and annual salads that are harvested daily can be planted along the front edge nearest to the door. Vegetables that are harvested often, but not daily, can grow behind those, such as peas, French beans or courgettes. Plants are placed according to frequency of harvest until you come to those only harvested once a year such as onions, potatoes, apples or willow, which are placed right at the back. By applying zoning to our small space, we can make them work really efficiently, which in the end makes them more enjoyable and more likely to draw us out to tend them. If you throw in some keyhole beds too, you can create a really attractive and functional garden. There are always those hard-to-reach corners that can be left unmanaged, as a sanctuary for wildlife. Even in the smallest garden it's important to leave room for nature to do its own thing.

I believe forest gardening to be a very accessible way many people can practice permaculture at home, even with a tiny space, but permaculture is not just a set of farming or gardening techniques. It has grown to encompass the whole of human habitation from food growing and eco-homes to economics, health and transport. Permaculture design can be applied to any aspect of life, not just gardens. I have used it to design my garden, my business, my home, family life and many other things. This book is focused on forest gardening but will still encompass all ethics as the garden needs to meet all our needs, not just be a food producer. By now you should have an understanding of what a forest garden is, an understanding of why growing a diverse community of plants is beneficial to us and the planet and some ideas about how this might be possible on a small scale. Having covered the what and the why, we need to get to grips with the how; the next chapter will guide you through the first steps on the permaculture design process.

Wooded areas too shady for food growing can be kept as wild as possible and form zone 5

Unmanaged areas are havens for wildlife such as this ground nesting bee

Poppy harvesting annual salads in year 1

CHAPTER 3

How to Design Your Small-scale Forest Garden

So why use a design process?

I love experimenting, throwing caution to the wind and changing things about, so you may be wondering why I am advocating using a structured design process, especially as you may be chomping at the bit to get some plants in the ground. When I began the yard design I had beds of bare soil and the perfectly understandable desire to get something edible going. Ideally as a designer I always suggest a full year of observation to really understand the microclimates and features of your site as they change through the seasons. So in year 1 I sowed a mixture of annual salads, herbs and flowers.

This way I had a whole year of colour and food whilst making these vital observations. I could note where it was a bit too shady for the tomatoes, too hot and dry for the lettuce and how we liked to move around the yard (desire lines). Where do I like to sit? What activities take place over the course of a year? When gardening with perennials, especially trees and shrubs, it is more difficult to go back later and make changes. Certainly hard landscaping features such as walls, paving and paths cannot easily be tweaked later. You want to get the basic layout right the first time, so careful design and planning is required. Permaculture design is also about creating beneficial relationships between elements within the garden, which may be overlooked when missing out the analysis stage of designing.

I find the design process really empowering as I can start a project with scant relevant knowledge and still come up with a workable design. Don't let the fact that you have very little prior knowledge put you off tackling a project. I aspire to build a homemade wind turbine and fit small solar panels to the shed; I have no idea how to do either yet but by following the permaculture design process outlined below I will find solutions.

I have broken the design process down into small steps so you can feel confident about following it, concentrating your energy on the content of the design. Recording your notes/thoughts doesn't have to be complicated. You may like to type it up, dictate it on your phone or simply take pictures and scribble notes. Whatever works for you is fine; the aim is to create something that is useful for you and is enjoyable enough that you want to keep going until you have a workable design. I enjoy beautiful notebooks with lots of scribbled mind maps, sketches and photos. My husband Andrew prefers spreadsheets and dictating notes on his phone. Just make sure everything is in one place (catch and store energy) so you don't use all your precious design time looking for things. I have written that as if all my notes are carefully put in one notebook and not some in a bag, some in the van, some by the bed and mixed up with my business accounts, but it's something to aim for.

▶ Starting with annuals and small herbs in year 1 means you can still move things around

Brainstorming in my notebook, making a wish list and recording ideas

The design process

Survey stage: observe what is there, collect data

This stage is all about observation. Try as much as you can not to make any decisions during this stage. It can be useful to include any ideas as brainstorming here, rather than as fixed ideas. Collect these ideas and you can revisit them during the analysis phase to see if they will work. I have often thought I knew exactly what I wanted at the beginning and followed the design process anyway to see if any other ideas came up. The end result was a totally different, much more successful product.

Rather than fixing ideas during the survey, I like to begin by establishing my aim. This helps to decide which information you need to gather, but it's still good to keep an open mind at this point. I find this works best as a single sentence, nothing too detailed yet. Past aims have included 'A yard edible polyculture with ornamental elements, family friendly', 'Patch of forest garden to include bird hide', 'Forest garden for bee forage with other wildlife habitat'. Don't worry if yours is currently just 'Small-scale forest garden', that is what the process is for, and it will help you make those decisions.

Brainstorm

A simple task is to pick out some key words; this can often help to pin down those abstract thoughts and dreams we have about what we are trying to achieve. When designing the yard, I began with a very uninspiring ocean of stone flags, cobbles and bare soil. I had visions of lush edible plants spilling out over the paving and up over arches, splashes of colour from flowers, birds hopping around, children playing and foraging and me sipping coffee in the sunshine. I simplified this to 'Abundant food', 'Wildlife habitat', 'Flowers', 'Social space', 'Fun'.

Gather any other images or plant lists, using them as a wish list rather than a finalised list. Go wild and be as imaginative as you can; I would love lemons and a living willow sculpture. These may not be possible but dream a little; there is plenty of time to discount these ideas later but they may spark another idea that is possible.

Base map

An accurate base map helps us see the true shape of our garden; it's seldom the shape we think it is. It allows accurate planning for siting different features, purchasing materials and plants, saving costly mistakes. It's too late once the shed has arrived and you realise it takes up the space for the flowerbed too. The technical side of creating a base map can sound so off-putting for some that the design never gets started. If you feel this way, maybe a rough sketch with the minimum of measurements is enough, if it means you can then get onto the bits you find more rewarding.

Drawing a base map using triangulation (pinpointing features on your map measuring from two fixed points) is easier than you think; invite someone over for moral support over tea and cake if it helps. It is much easier with someone to hold the other end of the tape measure and to remind you what measurement it was you just took. Pick two base points,

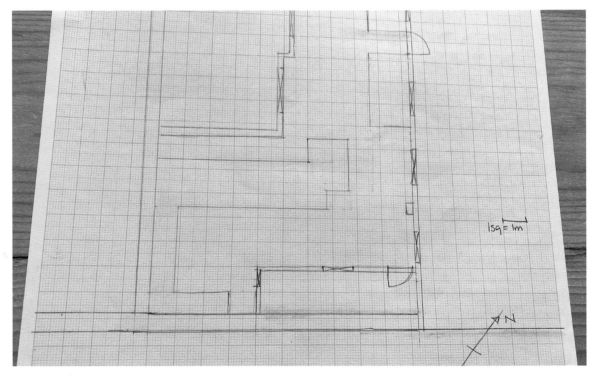

Base map of my yard

usually the corners of a building facing the garden, but best if they are easy to access to measure all other points in the garden. From each of these two points, A and B, measure to all other fixed points and features in the garden: the ends of walls, trees if they are large features, the boundaries etc. If the boundary is curved, pick a series of points along this and join them up later on paper. I am a very visual person so I like to sketch a rough base map and mark on each point so I can work out later if I have taken a wrong measurement. Measure twice now and save yourself having to repeat the process later on.

A great scale for the average sized garden is 1:50, so 1cm on your plan represents 50cm in your garden. Take your measurement from the garden and divide it by 50 to get the figure for the plan; 275cm (2.75m) in the garden becomes 275/50 = 5.5cm on the plan. A small garden could use 1:25 so 1cm on paper represents 25cm in the garden; this allows for more detail to be added.

It is worth the effort as once you have the base map, you can use it to record all sorts of other information during the survey stage, to 'play with placements' during the analysis stage, as well as for the final design draw-up. Use tracing paper or photocopies to allow you to use the same base map many times. If you have the skills, there are plenty of apps and programs online to draw your base map in 3D on your computer or phone.

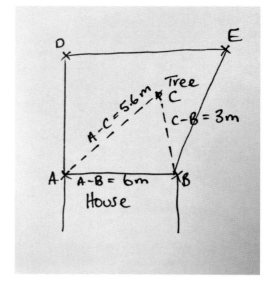

▲ Measuring for a base map using triangulation

▶ Client interview and site survey mind maps: black text is the template which I photocopy so I can use again for each different site

Client interview/Design questionnaire

Permaculture is all about a holistic approach, the relationship between person and garden (and the wider environment and planet). I use a couple of templates to carry out a client interview and a site survey; both are equally important. Using templates helps to ensure we have remembered to gather all the information we require. By articulating and putting down on paper your thoughts and feelings, you are starting to get things clear in your mind, perhaps considering things you hadn't thought were important but are interlinked; as the gardener you are fundamental to the garden.

Site survey

What's currently there? Often I am taking the measurements for the base map at the same time as doing the survey so I like to sketch out a rough plan to add notes to. If it helps, copy the templates from the photo; feel free to tweak it to suit your needs. I love using templates as I often get carried away looking at the details of a site and forget to capture all the information I need.

Once you have sketched the garden, you can start adding notes such as boggy patch, sunny wall, existing apple tree etc. Capture as many details as

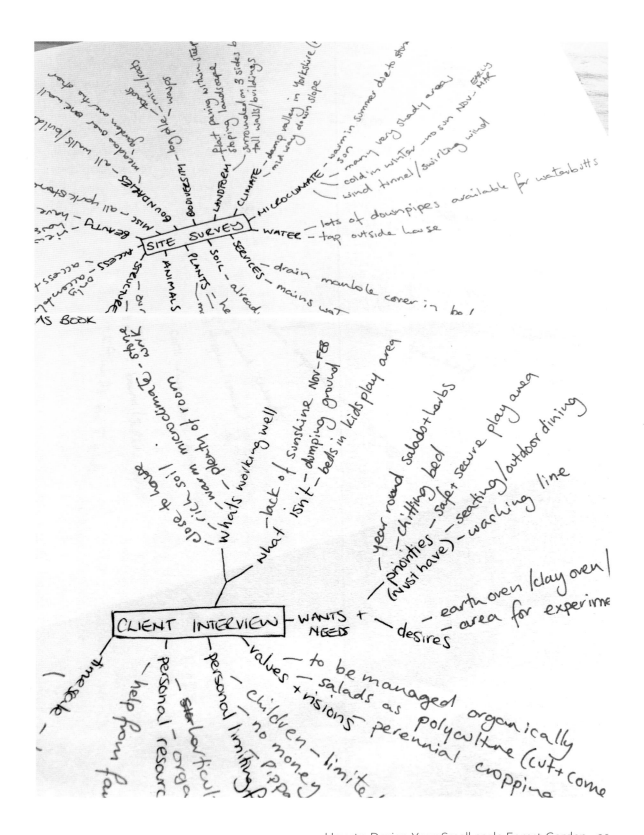

SITE SURVEY

- MICROCLIMATE — warm in summer due to sun
  - many very shady area
  - cold in winter — no sun Nov – early Mar
  - wind tunnel/swirling wind
- WATER — lots of downpipes available for waterbutts
  - tap outside house
- SERVICES — drain manhole cover in bol
  - mains wat
- SOIL — alread
- PLANTS — he
- ANIMALS
- STRUCTURE — on ou
- ACCESS — accessiba
- BEAUTY — have
- MISC — all york sto
- BOUNDARIES — all walls/buildi
  - meadow over the wall
  - garden over the fence
  - schem Gap — hus
  - thorn — apple
  - sports (poa) mint [pool]
- LANDFORM — flat
  - sloping landscape
  - giving within itse
  - surrounded on 3 sides b
  - tall walls/buildings
  - damp valley in Yorkshire (
  - mid way down slope
- CLIMATE
- AS BOOK

CLIENT INTERVIEW

- WANTS + NEEDS
  - desires — earth oven /clay oven /
    - area for experime
  - priorities (must have) — year round salads + herbs
    - chitting bed
    - safe + secure play area
    - seating/outdoor dining
    - washing line
  - what isn't — dumping ground
    - beds in kids play area
    - lack of sunshine Nov – Feb
  - whats working well
    - close to house
    - plenty of microclimate
    - worm rich soil
  - values + visions — to be managed organically
    - salads — polyculture (cut + come
    - perennial cropping
    - children — limite
    - no money pippa
    - personal limitat
    - site hortical — orga
    - personal resourc
    - help from fa
  - timescale

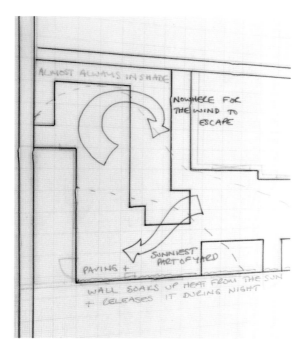

Overlay on tracing paper of sector analysis to show wind direction, sunlight and microclimate details

My dream of abundance came true

you can, and take lots of photos. I often take short video clips on my phone as it helps me to remember the garden in 3D when I'm sat inside putting things down on paper. Keen observation is key to this task; the more you can take note of the microclimate and special features of the site, the more successful the final garden will be. If you try to plant an apple on a north facing wall in wet soil, you will be sorely disappointed; if on the other hand you used the information about that spot to see the opportunities for shade-loving plants that tolerate damp soils, you could plant gooseberry instead.

Try to observe the less tangible things, such as energy flows, within the space and mark them down on your sketch. Where does the prevailing wind blow? How do you move through the garden? How does water move through or gather in the garden? All these will be really important when analysing what elements to include in your design and where you can place them.

Vision board – let yourself dream

I love to look through pictures of other gardens and visualise how I can reimagine them in my own space; it's even better to go and visit them. If you enjoy it, create a mood board for your forest garden. Would you love to see willow sculpture? A small wind turbine? A border full of abundant fruit trees and billowing flowers? Let your imagination run wild; just remember to capture it in some way. I get a lot of enjoyment (another important yield to remember) from artistically piecing my ideas together on a board or in a scrapbook; it is the artist in me. My husband on the other hand would much rather type up ideas in a spreadsheet. Both are equally valid; find what works for you. This is a time to gather ideas/hopes/dreams without the constraints of whether or not they could become a reality. You can worry about that in the next stage of the design cycle, the analysis phase.

	Positive	Negative	Interesting
Annual Vegetables	High yields	Alot of work to sow + feed+weed	Some self-seed
Fruit	Low maintenace Flowers for insects Attractive	Take up alot of space	Plants could go under canopy
Perennial vegetables	Come back each year Low maintenance	Less choice Often less tasty	Could mix in with perennial flowerbeds

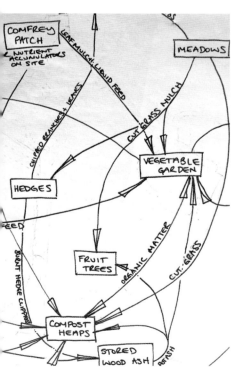

▲ P.n.i analysis from my notebook when deciding what to grow in the yard

▼ Closing the fertility loop by finding uses for outputs

Analysis phase: weigh up all the information

Hopefully during the survey stage you have generated a lot of information to get cracking with the analysis. This stage is all about sorting through the ideas and information, weighing up the pros and cons and deciding what is possible. There are plenty of tools to help us along, so once again we can concentrate on the design not the process. A great place to start is to do a p.n.i (positive, negative, interesting/opportunities) analysis for any elements you have identified you would like in the garden. This can help to make decisions such as apple vs plum, paving vs decking, or may help you decide whether to include an element at all, such as a pond or firepit.

This process will produce different answers for different people; some things I may think of as a positive quality, such as a tree providing shade to shelter me from full sun, may be a negative for sun worshippers.

Input/output analysis

This helps with closing the loop in a system so you are not wasting anything. Can you make the outputs of one element into an input of another element?

McHarg exclusion method

Sometimes there appears to be too many choices. Starting to look at where something can't go helps to focus in on where it can. Start with the most permanent structures or elements first. The shed can't go on the slope or in front of the kitchen window and it makes no sense to put it right in the middle of the growing area, so what options are you left with?

Random assembly

Often we can get stuck in conventional thinking when deciding how to piece together our designs. Random assembly frees us from this burden by generating unusual pairings for us to consider. Looking at the possible relationships of these elements in our system (the garden) can help us to see efficiencies in time, space and energy. Begin by writing each element of your design, such as pond, vegetables, fruit tree, water butt, greenhouse, on individual pieces of paper. On more pieces write placements such as: on, in, under, next to, over. Place these face down in two piles and pick two elements and one placement and try to think of the benefits to this pairing, however ludicrous it may seem. You may be surprised with what you come up with. The outcome of this process is to make sure you have considered all possible placements and beneficial relationships, even those you would never have considered yourself. Make sure to keep a note of the interesting or useful pairings or ideas.

Functions/systems/elements

Two further permaculture principles not listed earlier are 'Each element performs multiple functions' and 'Each important function is supported by multiple elements'. Ideally we want each element within our garden to perform as many functions as possible. This creates an efficient and resilient garden which will in turn give increased yields for reduced effort. Some of your functions may include food production, beauty, irrigation, windbreaks and recreation. Revisit the seven Fs if you are feeling stuck.

Consider the systems you may use to fulfil the required function. For food production would you like to include annual vegetables as well as your forest garden, and could this include animals such as chickens? Meeting the water needs of the garden could include a water butt and could include reducing water use. Could your windbreak be an edible hedge or a green wall, thereby fulfilling two functions?

Break this down again into the individual elements to start to piece together the details of what will be included in your final design. When you get to the point of deciding which elements to keep and which to leave out, choose those which can fulfil the most functions. Mulch can reduce weeding, preserve moisture and feed the soil. Water butts can collect water and if sited in a greenhouse can help to regulate the temperature and prevent frost. Lastly I believe there is also room to put something in just because you love it; you may just have to live with its inefficiencies.

Growing pumpkins in a large planter up the house wall provides food, shades the house and our seating area, and the compost from the planter becomes mulch for the garden

Using to scale, cut out circles
to come up with a collaborative
community forest garden design

Play with placements

Cut out shapes for each element, ideally to scale – think about how each element would relate to and work with those around it, use some of the information you gained from the p.n.i., input/output analysis and functions analysis to create beneficial relationships. Could the compost heap go near the chickens so you don't have to go too far when cleaning them out? If you place the comfrey next to the compost it can mop up any nutrients that leach down into the soil. This process really helps you to understand how elements work together.

At this stage it is really helpful to reflect upon the ethics and principles to check that each element within the garden fits within the guiding principles of permaculture. Some may not seem relevant but others may spark new thinking and ideas to help decide what to include, how to source the materials and long-term goals. Hopefully after using some of these tools and analysing the information from the survey you will have filtered out ideas that won't work, whether practically, financially or for other reasons. By the end of the analysis phase you should have pinned down the main elements you want within the garden: Which areas are for plants? Do you need seating/socialising space? Do you need a shed and where is it best to site it? All this information sorting means you are ready to put things together in a more formal way in the design stage.

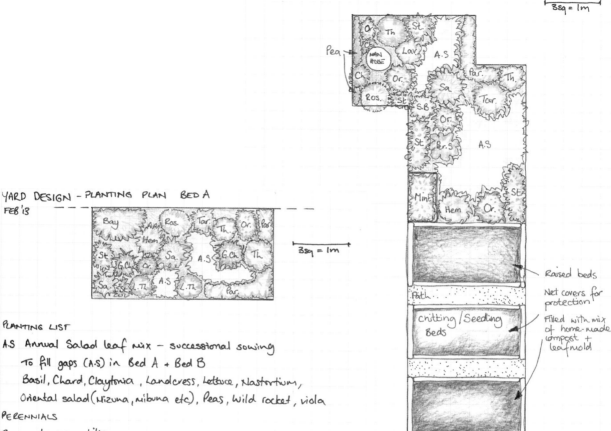

YARD DESIGN - PLANTING PLAN BED B
FEB '13

3sq = 1m

YARD DESIGN - PLANTING PLAN BED A
FEB '13

3sq = 1m

Raised beds

Net covers for protection

Filled with mix of home-made compost + leafmold

Path

Chitting / Seedling Beds

PLANTING LIST

A.S Annual Salad leaf mix - successional sowing
     To fill gaps (A.S) in Bed A + Bed B
     Basil, Chard, Claytonia , Landcress, Lettuce, Nastortium,
     Oriental salad (Mizuna, mibuna etc), Peas, Wild rocket, viola

PERENNIALS

Bay - Laurus nobilis
Ch. - Chives, Allium schoenoprasum
G.Ch - Garlic chives, Allium tuberosum
F.   - Fennel , Foeniculum vulgare
Hem. - Hemerocallis sp.
Mint - Mentha sp.
Or. - Oregano , Oreganum vulgare cultivars
Par. - Parsley, Petroselinum crispum
Sa   - Sage , Salvia sp.
S.B - Salad Burnet, Sanguisorba minor
Tar - Tarragon, Artemisia dracunulus var. sativa
Th   - Thyme (L.Th - Lemon Thyme) Thymus vulgaris
St   - Strawberry (Yellow Alpine) Fragaria vesca - unknown Yellow cultivar
Ros - Rosemary - Rosmarinus officinalis
W.G - Wild Garlic, Allium ursinum - bulbs dotted throughout

◄ Bed A final design for the yard polyculture

▲ Bed B final design; both beds have changed dramatically since these first designs with additional layers in the form of fruit trees, kale and shrubs

◄ A 3 x 3m forest garden design I did for Horton Community Farm. Trained fruit maximises the light available for other layers.

Scale 1:20

3m x 3m FOREST GARDEN
PDC 2011 Synergy

Design stage: putting it all together

The design stage is all about pinning down and recording the detail. The first level of detail is to create a bubble diagram on the base map, or using the paper shapes from the 'playing with placements' stage by sticking them in a permanent position. This level of detail may be enough for you; I like to then do a neat line drawing of the final design on which I can include the individual plants. However I also often miss the detailed planting plan phase. I decide where the main structural plants will go in the tree and shrub layers, then I create a list of plants for the understory layers, which I lay out in situ when I am ready to plant them, moving them around until I'm happy. It may help to do a more detailed planting plan including each individual plant if you are new to gardening or are unsure of the spread of each plant. This can also be helpful to refer to if something dies or you forget what it is.

Once you have your final design you can work on creating a timetable for preparing the site, sourcing materials and working out which tasks need undertaking and the order in which to do them. Once you have placed the main elements and larger trees, you can start to focus on a more detailed level of design, the plants that will make up lower layer polyculture. Planting, observation and maintenance phases will be covered in Chapter 6.

Guild based around two pears in a narrow border 1.5m wide

CHAPTER 4

Designing Polycultures and Guilds

Designing a whole forest garden is pretty daunting. If we take the concept of a multi-layered edible ecosystem we can break it down into smaller parts, i.e. the shady corner, the sunny wall, the seating area, the boggy bit. Break this down further into small groupings of plants called guilds and it suddenly seems more manageable.

What is a polyculture?

A polyculture is a combination of plants growing in the same space. This could be a simple mix of two or three annual plants such as tomatoes, lettuce and carrots or a complex woody perennial food system in the form of a forest garden. A polyculture is designed so that each plant can grow well in combination. It can be a lot more basic than a guild.

▲ A simple polyculture of lettuce, wild strawberries and garlic

▶ A guild with perennial kale 'Taunton Deane' as the canopy, flowering plants for pollinators, clover for fixing nitrogen, herbs and perennial vegetables for food and groundcover plants

What is a guild?

A guild is a community of plants carefully chosen to complement each other by fulfilling different functions, creating a harmonious (in our case small-scale) ecosystem. The idea is to maximise cooperation between plants whilst minimising competition. It is a step up from companion planting, which pairs plants for beneficial effects such as attracting pollinators or repelling pests. Within any garden or natural ecosystem there are always elements which limit growth,

a constant battle for resources of water, light and nutrients. In our garden, we need to balance this competition through careful design. If we do a good job, our community of plants should find a good balance and be able to maintain itself to a large extent. It may sound daunting but for me, it has been more of a journey of discovering which plants pair well. Don't expect to get this amazing balanced ecosystem with your first attempt. It's a living being and by gardening it, you will soon be able to tell if something is out of balance.

Where to begin when designing a guild?

A fruiting tree or shrub is usually the primary focus and the guild is built around this, working outwards and downwards through the different layers. Not all seven forest garden layers need to be included, it is just an ideal and the focus may not always be a tree; it could be a perennial kale trained as a tree or a patch of Jerusalem artichokes. Plants within a guild perform different functions, some plants providing multiple benefits. During your survey stage, decide the primary function of your garden (listed below) and select plants that will meet those needs.

The main functions are:

- Food for human use
- Pollinator attractors
- Nitrogen fixers
- Dynamic accumulators
- Pest control

I love including *Brunnera macrophylla* (great forget-me-not) for its early flowers for pollinators which serves no other purpose, unless you include the joy it gives me as a function. In fact I often include plants just for their aesthetic value as this is a really important function of plants for me. I would argue that 'looking beautiful' is another main function; it is after all the function of the majority of domestic gardens in the UK. You can have a forest garden whose primary function is as a beautiful setting to spend time in and also happens to produce food and provide habitat for wildlife. As the people who will be creating and maintaining our forest gardens, we must not forget the people care side; beautiful gardens are good for the soul.

Back of the envelope design for a small guild

Brunnera macrophylla 'Hadspen Cream' with its lovely blue flowers

Food for human use

This is a fairly obvious function of a forest garden, often named a food forest, as it is a way to grow food that mimics how a forest grows. Ideally to maximise our yields, every plant within the garden would produce some kind of edible element. In reality this can be very limiting. I have tried it but found there were so many other exciting plants I was itching to grow and in the end I felt huge relief at breaking free from this constraint I had set myself. It makes sense for the tree element of your guild to be edible. Most fruit trees have beautiful blossoms and the bonus of autumn interest in the form of fruit. The size of your space will limit this choice. A walnut will grow huge and its roots release juglone into the soil which reduces the vigour of most other plants trying to grow near it. This would be fine in a large forest garden where there is space for it to grow without many layers below it. In a small space, it is best to avoid it.

Apples, pears, cherries and plums are the usual fruit I would expect to see as the tree element of a guild. When deciding, you could do a positive/negative/interesting analysis.

Once you have decided which type of fruit or nut to grow, there is still a bewildering choice of varieties. Other than the consideration of size discussed in Chapter 1, it is impossible for me to narrow this down much as personal choice is so important. Even within our own garden my husband and I argue over variety. I like a sweet apple whereas my husband, Andrew, prefers them so acidic it makes me wince. Eating fruit plucked fresh from the tree is a wonderful experience, made more special if the flavour is delectable. If we know a fruit is bland, we may end up not bothering to harvest it. If the flavour is something special, we will savour every last mouthful. Many nurseries and community orchards have tasting days in the autumn so you can try out many different varieties. It is well worth waiting as this tree will be there for the long haul so you want to get it right. If you really are desperate to get planting, look on a few different sites to get an overall idea of the flavour before committing.

After flavour, the next crucial quality is pest and disease resistance. I have tasted some wonderful apples but a few years after planting, I had to cut them down and burn them due to canker. This is a tragedy when you have made the effort to plant, protect and prune them. Once you have narrowed down flavour, you can make a list of your desired varieties and discard any that are prone to disease. If you are still unsure it is worth contacting a local nursery specialising in fruit to discuss your requirements. They should be able to tell you what grows well in your area and meets your needs for size, flavour and disease resistance.

Another important factor to remember is that most fruit needs a compatible pollinator, meaning one that will flower at the same time as your

Edible hawthorn and crab apple, tasty in jellies but multiple seeds in each fruit make the hawthorn difficult to eat raw

fruit tree, to cross-pollinate. Some plants are classed as self-fertile but will still crop better if cross-pollinated.

In our yard I have two pears that are both a variety called 'Durondeau', so I still need another to cross pollinate. Trees of the same variety are genetically identical clones and can't cross. I don't have room for a third pear and the nearest pear of another variety is quite a way away. We have found a handy technique to solve this problem. We cut a small branch from a different variety of pear (hopefully you have a friend or relative with a suitable pear) which is flowering at the same time as the 'Durondeau'. A jam jar is then half filled with water, tied to the 'Durondeau' and the branch placed into the jar. As pollinating insects buzz around they visit the flowers of both the tree and the cut branch, transferring pollen from one to the other. Since doing this our pear crop has more than doubled. When your tree is flowering, look around for others in your area or ask around to find a suitable branch. Just make sure it is not the same variety as the one you already have. This technique will work for any fruit tree. Flowers will last several days with water in the jar; this should be long enough to get decent pollination.

Organic apples and pears are getting much more common. On the school run there is a house that puts

▲ Hanging a different variety of pear in the tree to aid cross-pollination

▶ Canopy layers of bay (*Laurus nobilis*) and pear are planted against the wall to give space for herbs and fruiting shrubs. Flowering plants such as geranium 'Rozanne' and delphinium give colour and food for pollinators.

Wild strawberry keeping the weeds down
around herbs on the edges of the forest garden

out apples to take for a small donation to charity; I often feel dismayed to see local trees with fruit lying on the ground as no one wants it. Bearing this in mind you may decide something like a cherry would give a more valuable harvest. The main complaint I hear about cherries, and I have this problem myself, is that the birds always get them before they are fully ripe. The exception to this is a yellow cherry which fools the birds into thinking they are still unripe and they leave them alone. This means I actually have the privilege of eating them myself, and they are just as delicious as the red ones. There are quite a few

yellow cherries available such as 'Napoleon' and 'Donissens Gold'.

Other edible plants for the understories are listed at the end of the book. Use the templates and tools in earlier chapters to help you decide which to include, remembering to mostly include things you know you will like and throwing in some for experimentation and taste testing.

A guild is all about the plants doing a lot of the work you would normally do such as feeding, weeding and pest management. If we have a community of plants growing in a way they would in nature, we can start to move towards a more self-sustaining system. No one is out weeding, watering and feeding forests in nature; they have their own cycles. It is trickier to create this self-sustaining aspect in smaller settings where you are looking to maximise food crops as there is less room for the plants that fulfil the other functions. When deciding which plants to include in your guild it is beneficial to choose those that serve multiple functions. Alpine strawberries are a great groundcover, they look very pretty, their flowers attract insects and you get a yield of delicious jewel-like fruit, so we can tick four boxes.

Pollinator attractors

Pollinators do a vital job, and without them we would be in big trouble. The more flowers that are pollinated, the bigger our yields. An orchard of fruit trees will attract pollinating insects from far and wide due to the sheer amount of flowers. Insects expend less energy if they can gorge themselves without searching or travelling far. Our much smaller offering of flowers may not draw much of a crowd compared to a whole orchard. In an urban setting, with few gardens, there will naturally be a much lower number of pollinators as there is less habitat for them to feed, live and breed. As a result we need to make our garden as attractive as possible to entice them in. There may only be a short window in which your main fruit crops are flowering so if you can extend the window in which your garden is attractive to pollinators, they will already be present and simply move onto the newly opened blossom to feed.

Spring is such a wonderful time; the garden is starting to come alive with flowering plants. I love to design gardens that have something flowering every day of the year where possible. In my yard this begins with witch hazel (*Hamamelis* x *intermedia*) and snowdrops moving on to crocus and miniature daffodils. We may still be in hibernation mode in the cold, dark months of winter and early spring, but any days that are warm and dry enough, pollinators will be out looking for food. If we can provide some of that sweet nectar, they will hopefully remember our

Picking herbs and flowers to use in the house

Inula hoopsii attracts bees and butterflies

Hamamelis 'Diane' in the winter sunlight

Rudbeckia laciniata is fantastic for pollinators and is great at the back of a border to give height and colour

garden and keep coming back. Some of my absolute favourites are: crocus, whose bright colours always bring a smile to my face; grape hyacinth (*Muscari*), a floriferous small bulb that will grow happily in some shade; and great forget-me-not (*Brunnera macrophylla* 'Hadspen Cream'), a perennial forget-me-not flower of a beautiful fresh blue, flowering for ages and attracting a myriad of pollinators just at the right time for my pears in the yard. *Symphytum* 'Hidcote Blue' is a short comfrey that begins flowering in February; its delicate tightly packed coil of flowers begins to unfurl and it is still going strong in May. On a sunny day it is alive with bees and other pollinators creating an audible humming of activity. It does have a tendency to sprawl so needs to be kept in check, but it's worth it for the months of flowers. It will grow in the deepest shade so can be used in those tricky places where not much else will grow.

When choosing, try to find single flower varieties (with one or two layers of petals on each head) where the nectar and pollen is easily available for the insects, rather than the fancy double flowers with lots of ruffled petals. Breeding has meant the double flowers often have extra petals where the sexual organs (which hold the pollen and nectar) would have been so are no use to insects.

Nitrogen fixers

It seems like magic; these amazing plants form an association with (or in reality are infected by) bacteria which fix nitrogen gas from the air into a form of nitrogen the plants can use. This is fixed in their root nodules then released into the soil making it available to surrounding plants. Nitrogen is a vital nutrient for plant growth – it is associated with leafy growth – and low levels of nitrogen mean poor plant growth. On the flip side, too much nitrogen can make growth too lush and weak-rendering it vulnerable to pest and disease attack. By including nitrogen fixing plants in our forest garden guild, we can ensure there is a balanced supply. I will go into more detail about feeding the garden in Chapter 7.

Dynamic accumulators

Have a think about how nature fertilises in a woodland. At the end of the year trees shed their leaves, herbaceous plants die down and the organic matter is deposited on the ground. Each year a new layer is laid down on top of the previous year's. Worms may pull this matter down into the soil and it may get mixed by small creatures digging but most nutrients are leached (washed down) to lower layers and taken up by the plants to start the cycle again. Dynamic accumulators have deep roots which can draw up these nutrients as they wash down, storing them in their stems and leaves. As they die down in autumn/winter, these stored nutrients are deposited on the soil surface where they decompose, releasing the nutrients for other plants to use. They carry on the nutrient cycle and feed the garden.

Nitrogen fixation in plants is a proven scientific process, whereas the nutrient cycle of specific dynamic accumulator plants is not (to the best of my knowledge at the time of writing). This does not mean it doesn't work, just that the science of it is still unknown.

In smaller spaces, especially where growing in large planters where subsoil is inaccessible, there is a case for leaving out the dynamic accumulators as the competition and space taken up by the dynamic accumulators, many of whom are large, deep tap rooted perennials, may not be worth it. My belief is that all plants are dynamic accumulators, taking food from the soil, bringing it to the surface and decomposing, cycling the nutrients. The most important factor to consider is not removing all the dead foliage at the end of the year to allow nutrients and organic matter to return to the soil.

◄ The shrubs at the back are nitrogen fixing *Elaeagnus*; dandelions are dotted about

▼ The dandelion has a deep taproot to access nutrients deep in the soil. When they die down, they add some of these nutrients to the top layers of the soil.

Pest control

Many of the plants that attract pollinators will also attract beneficial insects. These beneficial insects are either predatory insects who hunt and eat the pests, or are parasitoid insects who lay their eggs in or on pests' eggs, larvae or adults. Dot these insect attracting plants around your forest garden to spread the beneficial effect over the whole area. Aromatic plants with strong smells are great for confusing pests of specific crops by masking the smell. Onions are often planted around carrots to deter carrot root fly, the hope being that the strong oniony smell will mask that of the carrots and hide them from the pests. Herbs such as chives, mint, rosemary, lemon balm and thyme are useful for this.

Creating habitat is also important for encouraging beneficial insects into the garden. I used to despise wasps and remove their nests if I found them until one year I noticed wasps visiting my kale. I was

Pigeons can destroy perennial brassicas, but by mixing it with other plants, they haven't managed to find it

entranced watching the wasps fly down and eat the caterpillars straight off my kale plants. This seems a much more efficient system than me having to hunt about and pick off any I find. I hardly have any problems with caterpillars on my brassicas now. Sprays, even the organic ones, are often broad spectrum meaning they will kill most insects not just the pest we want to eradicate. This means we are killing off the beneficial ones as well, weakening our defence. Planting to attract as many beneficials as possible and hoping their levels build up to a high enough level to deal with the pest is a much more natural and holistic strategy.

Weed control

Plants need their own space in which to grow without too much competition for water, light and nutrients. Take this to the extreme and you get my most hated planting style, oceans of bare soil between plants. Some gardens I visit during consultations have more soil than plants, and they wonder why weeds are such a problem. Bare soil will naturally try to become covered by vegetation as seeds that were previously dormant are now exposed to the light and, seeing their opportunity, will germinate and grow. This constant battle is a waste of time and energy. Ground-cover plants can do the work for us. They grow across the surface of the soil, excluding light and preventing the majority of weeds from germinating. The added bonus is that many have added functions such as bugle (*Ajuga reptans*) whose small spires of flowers are loved by bees, or clover which fixes nitrogen so feeds the plants whilst excluding the weeds. Bare soil is a missed opportunity you can't afford, especially in a small forest garden. Pathways can even be covered by tough ground covers like alpine strawberries, creeping thyme or even groundcover sedums like *Sedum reflexum* or *Sedum* 'Blue Carpet', further maximising your opportunities for planting.

Whichever plants you select, the aim is to end up with a mix of plants that will happily coexist with minimal input from yourself. If you can make the most of the plants' natural beneficial qualities, nature can do the hard work of looking after the garden for you. In addition to the functions listed above, plants provide shelter for each other, taller plants provide shade for lower layers or structures to climb up; the list goes on. I like to include two or three of each plant that I use a lot. This way the plants can be harvested in rotation, giving them time to recover. It also gives resilience. If one dies I still have one or two left.

I think it's important to point out that whilst careful research and planning are important to create a successful guild, it should not be a daunting barrier to getting started. I am a big advocate for the 'throw it all together and see what happens' approach. Once you have a list of the plants you would like to grow, experiment and see what works. The character and structure of the guild will change over time as some plants die off whilst others may be a bit too successful and start to take over, so think of your plan as a starting point, rather than a final plan set in stone for eternity. A book may say a plant has a spread of 45cm; in one garden with rich soil it may spread to 1m, in another with poor soil, only 25cm. I have always found it best to put things in and observe; this is the fastest way to learn the quirks of your garden.

It will really help to make the whole design for the forest garden seem less daunting if you can start with one guild. If it works, you can replicate the process around the rest of the space. Not all planting has to be an intricately designed guild including plants fulfilling all functions and layers. You may decide to opt for something much more simple like various currants under the other fruit trees, underplanted with mint and wild strawberries and some comfrey for nutrients. You can always add to this over time, designing the guild in increments rather than all in one go.

You should now have a fairly good idea of the functional plants you want to include in your forest garden. In the next chapter I will be advocating the importance of garden aesthetics. If our forest garden is beautiful as well as functional, not only are we more likely to continue growing our food this way and spending time in our garden but we can hope to inspire others to do the same.

▲ *Ajuga* spreads about and prevents weeds growing

▼ Polycultures can be grown in the smallest of spaces, even without access to soil

Forest garden in
yard at Fern Cottage

CHAPTER 5

Flower Power

t is my passion to convert as many gardeners as possible to forest gardeners. Coming from a background of ornamental horticulture, where aesthetics are the most important quality, it took me a while to realise the potential of forest gardens for everyone. In my quest to encourage more people to plant forest gardens in their small spaces, it's important to show they can be just as beautiful as their purely ornamental counterparts, with the added benefit of providing them with nutritious, organic food. The hope is these forest gardens will inspire our friends and neighbours to do the same. At our permaculture smallholding we have a few patches of more traditional forest garden dotted around an acre field. On open days, I find most people choosing to hang out in our yard, really inspired by the smaller scale mix of edible and ornamental as this is something they can replicate in their own gardens.

Edible flowers

The focus on flowers is the obvious element that makes a garden orna-mental. In a forest garden we aim to have multiple functions for each element so flowers that are both beautiful and edible fit the bill. Flowers have been used in cooking for thousands of years, and in the 16th and 17th century it was very fashionable, with pantries stuffed full of dried flowers for adding to soaps and powders, floral tonics and syrups and flower wines and liqueurs. Floral and herb salads were the centrepiece of feasts containing around 35 different ingredients, something we can aim for from our own forest gardens. Over the years edible flowers have fallen out of fashion, until now when they are enjoying a bit of a revival. They are not a staple crop in the forest garden but can add that extra flourish to a sweet or savoury dish, to really celebrate our home cooked food.

▲ Violas are great for decorating salads and cakes

▶ Forest garden patch in the field at Fern Cottage

Selecting which to choose

Most flowers in the garden are technically edible; it's about choosing those with a lovely flavour and as with any plant you include in your forest garden, tasting it first is the ideal. My favourites in my forest garden include lavender, *Hemerocallis* (daylily), viola, chives, thyme and garlic chives. I use them in salads every day when they are flowering and lavender scones are heavenly with some homemade gooseberry and elderflower jam and lashings of clotted cream. The flowers of herbs usu-ally have a similar but more subtle flavour than the leaves so make a great addition to salads where the leaf of the herb may be a bit overpowering.

When purchasing plants with edible flowers from non-organic sources, be aware they may have been sprayed with pesticides or fed with artificial

A green wall is a great way to grow many edible flowers in a small garden.
It keeps them off the ground so free from soil and away from slugs.

fertilisers not suitable for edibles. It is best to grow them on at home for three to six months before consuming the flowers, to reduce the risk of ingesting any residues. If you can, find an organic grower or ask a friend who grows organically for a clump from their garden. You can also grow from seed if you have the patience and space; it's so rewarding to sow a seed and nurture it to the point of harvest.

Harvesting

It is best to pick your flowers early on a dry day after the dew has dried off, when the plants still have a high water content but before temperatures rise enough to evaporate the essential oils. This will mean your flowers are dry but should still have plenty of fragrance and flavour. Ideally pick the flowers on the day you will be using them but if that is not possible, they store well in a sealed container in the fridge with a damp cloth to keep the humidity high. If they are a bit wilted by the time you need to use them, they can be floated in a bowl of cold water and they should perk up.

Usually it is only the petals that are eaten as other parts of the flower can be bitter and unpleasant to eat. Pollen can have health benefits but it can also cause an allergic reaction, so if you are serving to others it is best to remove the stamen; this is the male part of a flower which produces the pollen. Some flowers such as violas and honeysuckle blooms can be eaten whole and look lovely as a single flower atop a dainty cupcake, the kind you need to eat two of as they look so tempting. With large heads such as roses, hibiscus and sunflowers you simply pull the petals off; with rose petals it is best to remove the white part of the petal also as this can taste bitter. When harvesting larger umbel flower heads like elderflower, I use a fork in a combing action to remove the smaller flowers from the stem of the flower head as stems can add bitterness to cordials and wines. If foraging for edible flowers in the wild or public gardens, harvest from above dog's urine height and be aware you don't know what may have been sprayed onto the area.

Uses in the kitchen

Flowers make a great garnish but I like to celebrate the unique flavour and qualities of the flowers themselves. We have a family tradition to forage for elderflowers each year to make champagne and cordial. We have our favourite foraging spots around local cemeteries and walks and this year I have decided to plant a black-leaved elder in our yard, a *Sambucus* 'Black Beauty', so I can harvest its pink elderflowers and make pink champagne. It is like spring in a bottle and one of my most favourite flavours. We also freeze the flowers and add to gooseberry jam as the gooseberry ripens after the flowers have finished. Flowers can be used to flavour wines, liqueurs and to infuse oils. To infuse oils simply add a handful of flowers to a jar, fill to the top and leave for around three months. You then strain into a bottle to use in salad dressings and to drizzle over roasted vegetables. Water flavoured with flowers can also be used for sorbets and punches. Borage or viola flowers frozen in ice cubes add a special touch to any cocktail or summer drink.

I love this orange daylily in salads or for nibbling on whilst I am wandering around the garden

Daylilies are a versatile flower in the kitchen. Every part of the plant is edible, including its roots, but the flower is the focus for cooking. Its petals can be used in salads; I often pluck off a flower for a munch when pottering about the garden. The flower buds can be used whole in stir fries. You can even batter and deep fry the partially opened flowers. They also look beautiful and are available in a huge range of sizes and colours, each with its own slight varying flavour.

Dahlias come in a range of shapes, sizes and colours. I have never been a huge fan of dahlias as they conjure up images of pampered blooms with oceans of bare soil around each plant. That was until Andrew decided to grow a few and I discovered the petals are edible. Growing them amongst other herbs and perennial vegetables has given them an image makeover. Simply pull off the petals and sprinkle them in salads; the ones I have grown had a nice peppery taste but apparently they vary widely in flavour. Keep dead heading to prolong flowering. Few people realise they are related to Jerusalem artichoke so it is no surprise they also have edible tubers. Wild dahlia has been a food plant in its native areas of Central America for thousands of years. Since then they have been highly bred for their beautiful flowers rather than their edible roots. It seems all dahlia tubers are edible but the flavour varies from unpalatable to mildly sweet. A Swiss company, Lubera, has been developing a range of DeliDahlia for improved flavour. If you don't fancy trying the roots, the flowers still make a wonderful addition to the salad bowl.

Flowers can also be used as dyes for food and cloth. Calendula petals can add colour to ice cream and custard and can be used as a saffron substitute. You could grow and harvest your own saffron from the *Crocus sativus* bulb, although you will need around 150 bulbs to harvest just 1g of saffron, whereas calendula can grow in abundance and petals are easy to harvest.

I love making floral butter for spreading on hot toast to eat with soup. I use herb flowers such as chives, sage, basil and thyme. You simply pick the flowers and separate them from the stem; a fork can

Dahlia flowers come in a huge range of styles, sizes and colours from dwarf plants at 40cm to large plants at 1.2m

be handy for this. Using 5 tablespoons of flowers to every 150g butter, mash into the butter with a fork (I find this easiest on a flat surface), scrape into a tub then leave in the fridge. Wild garlic flowers and leaves can be used in this way and I freeze the butter to use in the summer and autumn.

Crystallising flowers is very simple to do whilst making the flowers look really jewel-like. You need egg white and super fine caster sugar. I put my caster sugar in a clean coffee grinder to make it really fine. Use a paint brush to cover the petals with egg white then lightly cover both sides with the sugar. Leave on baking paper in a warm dry place for several hours

Calendula petals added to herb butter give it a lovely orange colour. They can also be sprinkled over salads.

Wild strawberry flowers can decorate cakes or be dried for herbal teas

until crisp, then store in an airtight container. These should keep for a couple of days. If you want a vegan alternative or to make longer lasting crystallised flowers, use gum arabic (a natural gum from hardened tree sap) dissolved in colourless spirit, such as vodka, as a substitute for the egg. Using this method the flowers should keep for months in an airtight container.

The most popular way to consume flowers today is probably as herbal teas. They can be used fresh from the garden or dried to store for year-round use. Flowers such as chamomile, lavender and elderflower are commonly used in infusions. To dry, you can gather in bunches and hang upside down somewhere inside, ideally somewhere warm but not dusty or humid. Alternatively lay out individual blooms or petals on a piece of fabric stretched over a frame. Once dried, store in an airtight container such as a jar and store somewhere dark. I love to make my own herbal tea combinations by making several teapots, each of a different single flower or herb, then pouring different combinations into my cup until I find one I like. I can then put together a mix using the dried herbs and flowers to use out of season when they are not available in the garden. It is fun to do this with friends over a large slice of cake or some lavender scones.

Flowers for pollinators

The role of a flower is to attract pollinators so the flower can be fertilised, form seeds and spread them as far as possible to continue the existence of the species. As a species we have bred and selected flowers to be attractive to us and in the process have often bred flowers that are partially or even fully sterile, meaning they cannot form seed, as the pollen-producing anthers and nectaries have been replaced or obscured by more petals. For the horticultural industry this is fine as plants can be propagated by division or cuttings or hand pollinated, but it seems a shame to have flowers in the garden that are of no benefit to pollinators. When choosing plants for pollinators choose single flowers rather than double. Many roses don't have pollen or nectar available for insects due to the profusion of petals but there are some lovely single and semi-double flowered varieties available such as *Rosa* 'Ballerina', *Rosa spinosissima* and *Rosa moyesii* 'Geranium', the latter forming beautiful large edible hips.

Attracting pollinators into the garden is great for wildlife but is also important to increase fruit set on fruiting plants. The more pollinators you have in your garden at the time your fruit bushes and trees begin to flower, the more insects there are to visit and pollinate your fruit flowers. I like to include plenty of plants that flower in the month running up to and including the period of fruit blossom for this reason. Finding plants that flower at just the right time can be a bit of trial and error. When your fruit is blooming, have a look around the neighbourhood and see what is flowering and teaming with insects. Garden centres are not always a good indicator of this as often they are polytunnel grown or shipped in from abroad so flower earlier or later than they would in your own garden.

◄ *Inula hoopsii* below perennial kale gives plenty of colour to attract us and pollinators into the garden

▲▲ Crab apple blossom attracts pollinators and can cross-pollinate with apple; it also looks amazing

▲ I chose this orange geum to match the paintwork of the straw bale meeting room at Ecology Building Society

Extending the season

If you want to provide a real sanctuary for pollinators it is important to provide flowers for as much of the year as possible. This is a piece of cake in the summer months but much more challenging in the winter. Whenever I am designing a garden, whether specifically for wildlife or not, I always group plants into flowering seasons so I can be sure I am giving year-round interest and nectar. I split it into six groups, each covering two months. It gets a bit complicated when you split it down to 12 months as it is hard to pin down flowering to such an exact time period. Winter = December and January; early spring = February and March; spring = April and May; summer = June and July; early autumn = August and September; late autumn = October and November. Some flowers for the tricky winter/early spring include winter aconite (*Eranthis hyemalis*), hellebores, snowdrops, crocus, daffodils (*Narcissus*), winter flowering pansies, *Sarcococca*, witch hazel, *Mahonia* 'Winter Sun', primroses and *Daphne*.

◄ Spring bulbs add colour and interest when many plants are just starting to emerge from the soil

▲ *Rudbeckia* 'Goldstrum' gives a splash of bright yellow in the autumn and even flowers through mild frosts. I love how well it coordinates with this squash.

I like to use the dwarf daffodils as they are more natural looking than the larger daffodils and as they die down they don't look as messy. They don't compete for space as much as the larger daffodils as the foliage is more delicate so are perfect to grow amongst any of the edibles as they won't swamp them out. Just be careful to keep them away from edible alliums such as chives as the leaves can look very similar and you don't want to accidentally put daffodils in your salad. Ideally you should have roughly the same number of plants flowering in each section, although you will inevitably have less in the winter months as there is less choice. On those magical first warm sunny days of the year, there will be food available for any pollinators brave enough to venture out. At this point I would like to make the case for leaving dandelions in your garden. They are a really important food plant for bees and other pollinators early in the year when sources of nectar are scarce. We perceive them as a weed but they should be celebrated. You can make a wine or jam from the flowers and you can eat the blanched leaves if you can stand the bitter flavour.

It is really important to not use pesticides in your forest garden as you will kill off both the pests and the beneficial insects. This is also true of many of the organic sprays you can buy, including the soap sprays. This is because they are not specific to one pest but will kill any insect that comes into contact with them. A much better approach is to provide a healthy ecosystem where you encourage the predators of pests to manage the numbers for you (see Chapter 6). I will never forget the day I decided to go organic in my professional life as well as at home. I was watering a weed and feed solution onto a lawn where I was working as head gardener (I always hated doing this but the owners insisted on bowling green lawns), and as I was pouring this, a bee came out of nowhere to feed from a lawn daisy just as I dosed it in herbicides. That was the final straw. Luckily I now have clients who can appreciate the amazing variety of plants and wildlife that can live on an organically managed lawn. At home, all lawns have been replaced by polycultures.

How to fit in the ornamentals

As with any garden design, you are designing in both time and space. If we are looking to prioritise yields from our edible crops we need to find gaps in both space and time to fit in our flowering plants without reducing our edible yields too much. I include quite a few tall, thin perennials such as iris, *Camassias* and Dutch garlic (*Allium hollanicum*). Plants with spires such as delphiniums, *Veronicastrum* and foxglove (*Digitalis*) are like nectar skyscrapers making full use of the vertical space by covering the stem in tiny flowers. These can use the vertical space

Tall, upright plants such as this white bearded iris give flowers above the other layers without taking up too much space

Allium hollandicum dotted through the beds can look quite natural. They usually flower in May.

Clematis in the pear tree. Photo: Neil Chapman

without forming dense spreading clumps. I also love flowering ground covers such as bugle (*Ajuga*), London pride (*Saxifraga* x *urbium*) and *Viola sororia* 'Freckles', which can use the niche below larger edibles providing flowers and suppressing weeds. In my yard I have many self-seeded aquilegia which flower around May when other perennials are still quite small. Once they have flowered I cut the whole plant to the ground, foliage and all, to allow space and light for surrounding plants. They put out a second flush of foliage which grows happily beneath the leaf cover of other plants. Primulas are also great for this layering in time. *Primula rosea* have tiny bright pink flowers which start the year with a riot of colour as early as February or March, then get covered by the foliage of other plants until the following year. The beautiful purple globes of *Primula denticulata* are great for this too and *Primula beesiana* flowers for weeks on end with the flowering stem opening successive whorls of flowers whilst taking up minimal ground space.

Climbers are a very effective way to make the most of the vertical space. They can be grown through fruit trees, up obelisks or along trellis and walls. I have a lovely clematis which grows up through a trained pear tree in the yard. It has large flowers but is not too vigorous as to affect the health of the pear. Avoid *Clematis montana* as they are impossible to keep small and can kill a small tree. There are winter flowering clematis which could be grown through a fruit tree to provide valuable nectar and interest to the dormant trees. *Clematis cirrhosa* 'Wisley Beauty' and *Clematis napaulensis* would be perfect for this.

Some of my favourite parts of the yard are those in deep shade where very few edibles would thrive. I leave this area as my version of zone 5 in the permaculture site zones. It is left to itself and most years I don't even get round to cutting it back at the end of the year. This area is planted with shade-loving perennials. If you are loath to put plants without edible yields in your sunniest spots, why not fill your less productive, shady areas with flowering plants. I have a groundcover comfrey, *Symphytum* 'Hidcote Blue' which will grow in deep dry shade, such as under hedges and that difficult gap between the wall and the shed. Depending on the weather, this will flower continuously from February for a couple of months. The hum of the bees and hoverflies is audible from a distance as it is such a brilliant source of nectar. Great forget-me-not (*Brunnera macrophylla*) loves shade; its sprays of tiny blue flowers brighten up shady corners, which pairs well with the clouds of delicate purple flowers of dusky cranesbill (*Geranium phaeum* 'Samobor'). Japanese anemones are brilliant in shade as they provide colour and nectar at the end of the year, and white flowers such as *Anemone* x

Self-seeded foxgloves (*Digitalis*) are allowed to flower but most are removed before they set seed to prevent too many germinating and swamping out other plants

hybrida 'Honorine Jobert' really stand out in the shade under a fruit tree.

Without question, beautiful gardens lift the spirits and can have a healing effect. Green spaces are vital to our health and wellbeing and flowers can increase this effect. Scents and colours add to this almost magical effect; hot colours of reds, oranges and yellows can help to energise with cool colours like blues and purples helping to relax the mind. The importance of flowers in our forest gardens should not be underestimated.

Mulching a newly planted forest garden with chipped branches

CHAPTER 6

Planting and Maintenance

H opefully by now you should have a great plan and clear idea of what you want to grow and where to plant it. The next hurdle is how to fund and source all the plants needed to fill it. When I first started planning areas of my forest garden I was faced with the enormous expense of plants to realise my design. Browsing specialist fruit nursery catalogues online and leafing through their glossy brochures is a lovely way to pass the time but if your budget is tight and you are patient enough, propagation is a wonderful skill to learn and adds another yield to the implementation phase. Propagation is covered in more detail in Chapter 8, so for now I will cover practical issues with planting and sourcing plants.

Sourcing plants

Many of the perennial vegetables you may wish to grow in your forest garden are not available in your average local garden centre, which makes getting your hands on them a bit tricky. The best thing to do is search online to see which nurseries have the plants available to order. Many are only available during bareroot season (November-March), which is ideal really as that is the best time to plant them. Sometimes these specialist plants can seem expensive for what you get so you may decide to buy small and propagate or grow on before planting out. In the last few years I have noticed a surge in the number of nurseries offering unusual edible perennials for sale, but it is still a niche market so start looking in good time. Some of the large plant shows with their show gardens are a great place to go for that plant fix, and they also have nurseries from around the country selling specialist plants, increasingly

Plant fairs and specialist nurseries are great places to find edible plants and support small local businesses

Jostaberry we grew from a cutting, underplanted with garden mint.
Photo: Neil Chapman

those specialising in fruits and perennial herbs and vegetables. I purchased my perennial kale 'Panache' at RHS Tatton Park Flower Show around four years ago as a tiny cutting in a small pot and it is now dotted all around my garden.

In the past I have asked for permission to gather propagation material when visiting gardens, armed with secateurs for cuttings and bags for seeds. Ask around to see if anyone is digging out something you may want; much of my garden came from divisions or cuttings from friends. Social media is a great place for asking around, from cuttings of jostaberry and scion wood of heritage apples (for grafting onto a rootstock) to clumps of Babington leek. Seed swaps are becoming more widespread for those growing annual vegetables and I would love to see these happening for perennials. Be resourceful and stretch your budget as far as you can, always choosing local and sustainable options where possible. You can't get more sustainable than something dug up from a garden down the road.

Bareroot or containerised

When it comes to fruit trees and bushes I would always recommend bareroot where possible. This option is available during the plant's dormant period, roughly November to the end of March. This has several advantages.

- They are cheaper to post as you can pack several trees in a bundle without the bulk and weight of the pot and compost.
- The plants arrive at the right time of year to plant them with minimal aftercare; often the only irrigation they require is watering in after planting, then only in drought conditions for the first year.
- I have often seen pot-grown trees with a small amount of roots as they have been cut off to stuff into a pot. Buying bareroot means you usually get a bigger root ball, which is much better for the plant as it has more roots to access water and nutrients and to anchor itself.

Bareroot seedling trees 'heeled in' in pots with some compost until we are ready to plant them

The main advantage of pot-grown trees and shrubs is that they are available year round, so you can plant whenever you like. I feel this is outweighed by the big disadvantages of added expense and often being 'pot bound', meaning the roots have become congested in the pot and started to grow round and round in circles. Seedling plants put down a tap root, then put outside roots to anchor themselves in the ground. If they have spiralled around a pot, they are not very efficient anchors.

Pot-bound plant. Amazingly this shrub had been growing in the ground for several years but pulled straight out as the roots hadn't spread out.

Checking the level is correct when planting and firming the soil

Planting trees and shrubs

Square hole? Round hole? I really don't think it matters; what does matter is that you dig a large enough hole to spread out all the roots of the tree or shrub. This is less important with the lower growing herbaceous layers as they are low to the ground and need less anchoring. The depth of the hole is also vital. Too shallow and the plant will have roots exposed to the air and will also be poorly anchored in the ground. Too deep and the finer surface roots can suffocate and the base of the trunk/stem can rot. If you plant below the graft level on grafted trees and shrubs, the top scion can develop roots and bypass the rootstock giving unpredictable results as the rootstock will no longer be controlling the size or disease resistance of the variety. The point at the base of the stem or trunk where the roots begin should be just below soil level. With pot-grown plants this should be the level it was in the pot; with bareroot plants this should be obvious even without soil on the plants.

There are a few exceptions to this rule, such as blackcurrants which I like to plant deep as they root along the stem and form stronger bushes, and roses which I plant deeper than tradition would dictate as they are prone to wind rock if planted with their graft union above soil level. The theory behind planting them shallowly was to prevent the rose rootstock from suckering and taking over but I have found that rarely occurs.

Once planted, give a good water and stake trees if necessary. If fruit trees are on a dwarfing rootstock they are best staked as the tree won't produce a vigorous root system. Trees are best staked close to the ground, roughly 30-50cm above soil level with the stake at a 45-degree angle, with the top end of the post facing into the prevailing wind. This means as the wind blows, the tree still feels the effect so continues to put out roots to try to anchor itself. As the wind blows the tree, the force will be pushing the stake into the ground rather than pulling it out. I like to use old bicycle inner tubes cut into strips, first securing the tie to the post with a nail to keep it in

Planting herbs and small shrubs after laying out the pots

place, then tying round the trunk in a figure of eight to prevent the bark rubbing against the post.

Regardless of whether you have planted trees, shrubs or herbaceous perennials, a mulch is a must. Mulch means something to cover the soil that prevents weeds and reduces moisture loss. Black plastic is a very effective way to stop weeds growing but it will also prevent moisture and organic matter from reaching the soil. Weed suppressing membranes allow water through but still don't allow organic matter to be added to the soil, essential to keep it healthy and allow nutrients to be passed back into the nutrient cycle. In the long run the ideal is for groundcover plants to suppress the weeds and reduce evaporation but until this layer is established,

use an organic mulch such as chipped bark, straw or well-rotted manure. If you need to suppress already established weeds, a few layers of cardboard can go directly on top of the weeds with the mulch laid on top. This will exclude light, kill the weeds and will rot down, allowing organic matter to be added to the soil. A natural mulch will feed the soil and prevent the millions of seeds that have been lying dormant in your soil from springing into growth. It is a good idea to add a mulch every year, ideally something sourced locally or your own homemade compost and if you really feel you need to cut back and tidy up, put this into your compost heap, not the council garden waste bin. 'Produce no waste' means we must cycle everything back into the system.

Mulching with mineralised straw mulch 'strulch' using planks to ensure we don't compact the soil

Maintaining your forest garden

There is a tendency for some conventional garden designers to have a 'happily ever after' view of creating a garden. They plant and leave, seldom to return. Once the plants are all in and mulched, the garden is not finished, this is just the beginning. You can now begin the 'observe and interact' phase.

Your forest garden should require very little maintenance once established but careful observation is vital to long-term success. This is even more important in small-scale forest gardens because space is more precious. I like to carry out my observations with a cup of tea and some general pottering about. My yard forest garden takes very little time; I probably only spend around two afternoons a month doing any

actual maintenance but I like to have a good nosey around on an almost daily basis, especially when looking at what to harvest. An ideal in a permaculture garden is for the harvesting to be the only maintenance you do. This would be wonderful but not really realistic for most of us. A forest garden that is on our doorstep allows for much more regular maintenance than one on an allotment or a short drive away. I can pop out to gather some herbs and greenery for lunch and check on any badly behaved plants. Is the kale smothering out the sage? I can cut back the kale and steam it for tea. I may then notice that the strawberries have finally got ripe fruit on; they never make it as far as the house, but are enjoyed straight away.

Pruning wall-trained cordon apples and pears. They will need more pruning when trained this way but it is very satisfying once you know what you are doing.

You can create a forest garden to fit your available time and skill level. If you love gardening, you may wish to create a high maintenance forest garden with topiary and wall-trained fruit. Adding annuals into the mix can increase the maintenance. Or you can keep it really relaxed and low maintenance with lots of ground covers and less vigorous fruit that can manage without pruning every year. Once again I didn't manage to prune the pears in the yard this year but they will most likely still crop well. The most important thing is just to keep observing; this is when the best learning happens. If you are quite new to gardening, don't be afraid to experiment. Look things up online, in a book, watch a few video tutorials. During my first job as head gardener I didn't have a clue what I was doing most of the time but kept calm and looked it up in the *RHS Encyclopedia of Gardening* (in the days before smart phones). I learnt how to prune roses, how to train wisteria, and how to take cuttings. Of course none of the plants needing attention ever looked like they did in the book, so there was a certain amount of taking a deep breath, feeling the fear and doing it anyway. Let's just say I learnt a lot from my mistakes but it was such a brilliant time of learning to trust my intuition.

The main thing to do is remember to 'obtain a yield' from your observations by taking notes, photos and even videos. You can then refer to these notes later in the year when thinking about how to 'tweak' your garden or maybe just to reflect on how amazingly perfect it was and put your feet up as there is no intervention needed.

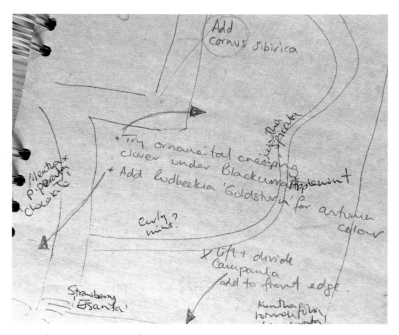

Observational notes for changes to make over the dormant season

Maintenance through the year
Cutting back without tidying up

As a minimum your maintenance regime should include harvesting, mulching and weeding if necessary. The usual garden ritual of cutting everything back and removing the debris in autumn to 'tidy up' is really counterproductive when you are trying to build a thriving ecology in the garden. You are destroying habitat each year and removing fertility and food for the worms. A better approach is to chop and drop. Take some shears and chop dead stems and foliage into small pieces and just leave on the bed to become the mulch. I tend to do this around January, once everything herbaceous has died down but before emerging bulbs get in the way. I like to remove long hollow stems whole before I start hacking away and bundle them up into a quiet corner of the garden. Often they contain hibernating insects who can help us in our fight against pests; they can emerge when they are ready without me disturbing them too much. I will usually add extra mulch to the garden at this point because I am cropping quite a few things in the garden so need to add fertility to make up for this (see Chapter 7).

I do some cutting back throughout the year as some plants may get too big and start swamping out other less vigorous specimens. This could simply be removing a few key large leaves or cutting the whole plant to the ground. Most herbaceous plants will survive a cut back even in the middle of summer. If this plant has edible leaves then you have a harvest from your maintenance.

Babington leek pushing through the chopped-up stems from the winter cut back

Observation and tweaking the design

Using your notes from the previous year, winter is a good time to make changes to the forest garden polyculture as most plants will be dormant and any relocated plants are more likely to survive and thrive. This year my main tweaks are to lift and divide clumps of viola 'Freckles' from one bed and golden oregano from another bed and spread them out along the edge of all three beds to give the yard a feeling of cohesion. My notes told me that last time I split the oregano in winter it just rotted, so this year I am trying again in April once the plant is in growth but before the foliage gets too big. Once plants are in active growth they are less likely to rot when divided.

A few things got killed off by a prolonged frost, even some hardy plants, so I am choosing to see the

huge gaps as an opportunity to try something new. I love globe artichokes; they are not a high yielding plant but have stunning architectural leaves and I have some ready that I grew from seed a couple of years ago. I love raspberries and whilst I may not have room for enough to collect for jam making, I would love some to forage whilst wandering through the garden. A variety called 'Ruby Beauty' is dwarf so I'm hoping it won't spread too much. My kale 'Panache', which was due a cut back due to its smothering habit, died completely and has left a huge bare space as it had already killed off some other plants, such as my garlic chives. This loss is similar to when a tree dies in woodland and suddenly the canopy opens, flooding the forest floor with light, changing the vegetation that can now live there. I need to guide this habitat succession to meet my needs otherwise weeds will fill this space. I can't quite decide what to replace it with so I'm going to put in some annuals such as peas and a courgette this year while I mull it over.

◄ While harvesting produce I can keep an eye on how all the plants are doing, cutting back those that are too vigorous or pulling out the odd weed

▼ New plants ready to go in as I rearrange some of the planting that has not done well

Pest and disease management

With careful design and management techniques, pest attacks should be minimised but prevention is always better than the cure. As mentioned in previous chapters, attracting beneficial predatory insects into the garden is the best way to tackle pest control. If you have a healthy army to defend your crops you have very little work to do yourself. In fact a certain level of pests could be viewed as essential to keep your beneficial predatory insects well fed so the odd greenfly here and there is not a problem. The main predators you want in your garden are:

Ladybirds

Probably one of the most recognisable predators in the garden, ladybirds are fantastic for controlling aphids (black and greenfly), scale insects and red spider mite and are often brought in for pest control in organic commercial greenhouses. They lay their eggs within colonies of aphids which become food for their larvae once hatched, each larvae eating up to 5,000 aphids. The best way to encourage these amazing insects into our garden is to leave some undisturbed areas within the forest garden, giving them somewhere to overwinter. I have observed evergreen groundcover comfrey swarming with ladybirds in the past. Piles of dead stems, twigs and logs would also be beneficial. Plants that can attract them include *Achillea*, *Ajuga* and *Tanacetum vulgare* (tansy).

Parasitic wasps

Unlike our common wasps, these small wasps do not sting. They are much more gruesome. They lay their eggs inside a host insect such as a cabbage white caterpillar, and once hatched, they eat their host alive from the inside out. They are brilliant for controlling caterpillars on brassicas, sawflies on gooseberries and aphids. Some plants to attract them include dill, *Astrantia*, lemon balm and *Tagetes tenuifolia* (marigold).

Lacewings

The adults look so delicate with their transparent wings but their larvae are voracious consumers of aphids and eggs of other insects, earning them the name 'aphid lions'. Some plants to attract them are coriander, dandelion, angelica and evergreen shrubs.

Wasps

We are taught from an early age to fear wasps and I have to admit I used to wonder what benefit they had to the ecosystem. That was until I watched one plucking cabbage white caterpillars from the perennial kale in my yard. They would fly down and carry them away. I later learned they hunt caterpillars to feed to their grubs, a wonderful way to control caterpillars without netting. If you find a nest and it is not a danger to anyone, it is best to leave it alone and be thankful for their help.

Hoverflies

These look similar to wasps but don't have the tiny waist that wasps have. The diet of the adults is pollen and nectar but the larvae feed on aphids and other insects. Plants to attract them include *Limnanthes douglasii* (poached egg plant), *Achillea* and *Helenium*.

Ground beetles

These amazing creatures are enthusiastic consumers of slugs, snails and vine weevil larvae so are certainly to be encouraged. Their habitat is log or stone piles, compost heaps and leaf litter, those wilder corners that never get tended, so this is a great excuse not to be too tidy.

One year the gooseberry in my fruit cage was completely stripped of its leaves by the gooseberry sawfly, whilst the same variety in the forest garden was lush and green with foliage. I did wonder whether the netting had prevented birds and other predators from eating the sawfly larvae whereas the forest garden is full of birds. I removed the bird netting, underplanted the fruit with forest garden ground covers and haven't had a problem since.

Ladybird pupae basking in the sun

Caterpillars attacking my perennial kale

It was a sad day when my kale tree died. I suspect it was prolonged frost leading to dehydration. The evergreen leaves continued to lose moisture but the frozen ground wouldn't allow it to take any more up.

Top tips to create a thriving community of beneficial insects

Flowers attract beneficials, especially those with open daisy-like heads or umbellifers. Try to extend the season of plants flowering in your forest garden.

Don't be too tidy. If you really don't like scruffy areas, make them into a feature. Your pile of stones or logs could be in a sculptural form. Shapes can be made from chicken wire and stuffed with leaves to provide habitat whilst staying contained.

Add water in the form of a small pond, bird bath or water feature. It doesn't have to be large but will meet another need of the insects meaning they are more likely to visit, stay and breed in your garden.

Leave small infestations of pests; they should soon be dealt with by your beneficials. If your garden was totally pest free there would be no food for your beneficial insects.

Don't use pesticides, even the organic ones. They are not specific to just the pests and will kill beneficials too, destroying all your hard work to build up a healthy ecosystem.

Disease prevention

If you can create a healthy ecosystem there should be minimal disease but this doesn't mean there will be no disease. There are a few ways you can help minimise disease in your forest garden. The plants most prone to disease tend to be the fruit trees and bushes. This may be because they have been bred for flavour and aesthetics at the expense of disease resistance. When selecting varieties I only choose those that are disease resistant, then I go by flavour as the second most important. If a plant is very ill, I will remove it as it is clearly not happy where it is. If you can remove diseased material quickly it can prevent it from spreading. Foliar sprays such as seaweed or aerated compost teas can boost vigour and help plants defend themselves against disease. Avoid any fungicidal sprays as you will damage the ecosystem of your garden and the plant will likely continue to be sickly. If you have been neglecting your soil, put down a good mulch, which might be enough to give a plant a boost. Avoid large amounts of really nitrogen-rich fertilisers as these can encourage weak lush growth which is more vulnerable.

You can get some great books and online resources to help you identify what pests or diseases you may have found but most then go on to advise pesticides and fungicides which are hugely detrimental to the ecosystem you are trying to create. Over time some plants will naturally die off; many are just not in the right place, so it makes more sense to remove them and try something else. I have certainly found that plants growing in a forest garden are much less likely to suffer from pest or disease attack, probably for all the reasons we have discussed so far. If you do need to remove something, don't see it as a failure, see it as an opportunity to try something new.

Don't tidy up too soon. I leave the stems until just before bulbs start to emerge.

This apple is free standing and its lower branches were trained downwards to get it to fruit lower, meaning it can be pruned to stay small

Pruning fruit trees and bushes

The scope of this book doesn't allow me to cover all pruning techniques you may need to know to maintain your forest garden. I would recommend reading a few books dedicated to fruit pruning, watching some videos, then finding a course or a forest garden or community orchard where you can have a go; this is the best way to learn. If you don't have the time or inclination to learn in this much detail, I hope the information here will mean your attempts are more informed, so less errors occur whilst you are giving it a go. In reality the dwarf fruit trees are nowhere near as vigorous as commercial orchard trees, so will likely require very little pruning other than to remove dead, diseased or dying branches. More technical pruning is required if you decide to wall-train fruit but even this is not complicated to maintain once you have achieved the basic framework during the first few years.

Knowing the basics and the reasons why we prune gives a really good grounding to then develop the technical skills. You are very unlikely to kill a tree from bad pruning. The worst you will do is reduce fruit yield for a few years and possibly end up with an oddly shaped plant.

Why prune?

Fruiting trees

The main reasons for pruning fruit trees are to control the overall size of the tree, increase yield and reduce pests and diseases. Pruning improves airflow, which reduces the risk of disease and increases light penetration, which increases maturing of fruit buds and ripening of fruit. When wall-training fruit, pruning keeps the tree to the desired shape whilst encouraging more fruiting spurs.

Fruiting bushes

Currants and gooseberries fruit best on the branches that are two or more years old. A good pruning routine after the third year is to take out about one third of the oldest branches every year so you should always have branches aged 1-3 years old. This is the most productive way to prune but in wilder parts of larger forest gardens I rarely prune fruit bushes and they produce plenty of fruit; they would simply produce more if I pruned them as it is the younger branches that have the best quality fruit. At harvest time you can cut off the entire three-year-old branch to harvest the fruit. This way you combine pruning and harvesting.

Raspberries are pruned differently depending on whether they are summer or autumn fruiting. Autumn fruiting raspberries can be cut right back to the ground once they have finished fruiting as the new canes will grow and fruit in the same year. Summer fruiting raspberries produce fruit on canes that grew the previous season, so cut out the canes that have fruited (these are the branched ones) and leave the younger canes. Tie them up to reduce damage over the winter.

Blackberries fruit on the previous season's growth, so cut back the fruited stems to the ground and leave the newer stems to fruit the following year. You can wall train blackberries if you don't have enough room to let them roam free. I have seen them trained in a spiral form on a trellis to get long growth into a very small space.

This is an overview of the ideal ways to maximise your yield, improve shape and reduce disease. In reality you will get fruit even if you leave them with no pruning, but in smaller spaces we want to get the highest yield we can from our forest garden so it is well worth developing your pruning skills.

▲ Use sharp, clean secateurs and cut just above a bud or leaf

▶ Thornless blackberry trained along wires. The fruited stems have been removed, the current stems will fruit this year and new stems will be tied in as they grow.

TIPS

Canker on an apple branch has been pruned off and will be burnt

When caring for young trees, remove all fruit for the first three years, to allow the tree to establish. It seems a waste but you are investing in the health and vigour of your tree for many decades to come.

Start by removing dead, diseased or dying wood, followed by crossing branches. Crossing branches compete for light and rubbing can cause wounds where infection can get in.

If renovating an old tree, don't remove too much growth at once; this will encourage a flush of new sappy growth called water sprouts, which will in turn need thinning by summer pruning. Remove one third of the total wood you want to take out, each year, for three years to avoid a proliferation of water sprouts.

Prune out small branches, stand back, assess the tree before then taking out anything bigger. Pruning should involve many careful observations.

Trees in the *Prunus* genus, including cherries, plums, gages and peaches should be pruned in late summer to avoid silverleaf infection, a highly destructive fungal disease.

In a natural woodland, a tree will put on lots of vertical growth until it reaches enough light to fruit, then it puts out more horizontal fruiting growth. When a branch is bent down to the horizontal, the combination of hormones that were telling the branch to reach for the light, switch to telling it to create fruiting growth. Once your tree is at your desired height, you can train branches to the horizontal by tying string to the end of the branch and securing the other end to the ground either with a rock or tent peg. This will encourage fruiting wood to develop.

Summary of the maintenance calendar

Late Winter	Harvest
	Cut back, ideally chop and drop, don't be too tidy
	Have a look at the notes from the previous years' observations and plan your tweaks
Early Spring	Harvest
	Make notes of observations
	Take out anything that has died
	Carry out your tweaks by moving plants about, lifting and dividing plants if necessary or adding new things
	Check for weeds if there are gaps
	Mulch
Spring/ Summer	Harvest
	Ongoing observation, take notes/photos
	Keep an eye out for pest or disease outbreaks
	Check competition between plants, cut back select plants if necessary
	Carry out late summer fruit pruning around July/ August if necessary
Autumn/ Winter	Harvest
	As always, make more observations and notes
	Carry out winter fruit pruning if necessary
	Cut back selectively where necessary

As you get to know your garden better you can design yourself a personalised maintenance calendar. Use the permaculture design process to help you put this together. The survey stage would be looking at what tasks you have identified during your observations, particular plants and their needs and any skills you have. Your analysis could look at when those tasks are best carried out, the benefits or drawbacks of certain tasks and any skills you may need to develop to meet the forest garden's needs. The more you maintain your garden, the more you will learn.

Laying a thick mulch of compost onto a bed with very thin topsoil

CHAPTER 7

The Soil Food Web and Natural Fertilisers

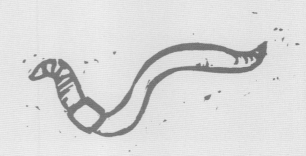

love soil; I get very excited by good soil. It is the foundation for a fantastic forest garden ecosystem. Much emphasis in forest gardening is given to creating a thriving community of plants but it is just as important to design a system where life thrives in the soil beneath them. Soil has a complex ecology and scientists are constantly making new discoveries in the field of plant health and soil fertility. You could technically grow your forest garden in pure sand and keep it watered and fed by a hydroponics system but this would be like feeding a human via a nutrient drip; not a great diet for long-term health and our body would soon become weak and vulnerable to pests and diseases. It would also require very high inputs. The best way to approach fertilising your forest garden is to feed the soil, not the plants. A healthy thriving soil food web in your garden will keep your plants fed and healthy. In nature it is the soil organisms which break down organic matter, making nutrients available to the plants. Modern agricultural practices such as tilling and use of herbicides and fungicides kill off the majority of soil life. With no soil organisms to pass nutrients to the crops, synthetic fertilisers are required to feed plants directly. Our job as forest gardeners is to assist soil organisms to look after our plants for us by keeping them well fed and protecting their habitat.

A healthy soil is teeming with life such as this centipede

The soil food web

This is a relatively recent term coined by soil expert Dr Elaine Ingham, a microbiologist and founder of the Soil Food Web School. It refers to the living organisms in the soil and how they all interact. Soil microbes such as bacteria, fungi, protozoa and algae have an important role in decomposing organic matter and making nutrients locked up in soil available to plants. Some can even help fix nitrogen and carbon from the air. Invertebrates such as nematodes, earthworms, springtails and moles also have important roles in a healthy soil as they aerate and pull organic matter down into it. In our forest garden, the aim is to help our soil be as close to 'wild' soil as it can be by not disturbing it. Organisms living in the soil often only survive at a specific depth or strata and in specific conditions, so if you dig soil you could be suffocating those from upper layers by burying them deeper and those from deeper down may die of exposure. One of the most important and helpful living organisms in our soil are fungal hyphae, like tiny threads forming a net-like structure in the soil. If soil is disturbed by digging, they are completely destroyed, which can have a devastating effect on the health of your soil food web (more about fungal hyphae later).

When digging we expend a lot of energy. By not digging and growing perennial crops we can minimise our energy inputs but still obtain a great yield. That said, if you are starting your forest garden on very poor, compacted soil or even subsoil, there is a good argument for a 'dig once' approach to get a decent amount of well-rotted organic matter into your soil. With perennial plantings such as fruit trees, shrubs and herbaceous perennials, you will not be digging again. It may be that there is very little soil life there to begin with, if all the air has been squeezed out of the soil and there is very little organic matter to support life. Most garden soil will not require digging but I have planted forest gardens where the initial soil was like digging concrete and was mostly gravel and subsoil. Nothing much would have thrived in there without an initial dig over and incorporation

Coppiced alder fixes nitrogen and releases it once it is coppiced, making it available to the plants around it

of well-rotted compost. After digging, this ground was left to settle for a couple of weeks before planting, which prevents plant roots sticking above the surface as the soil settles around them.

Bacteria

We tend to think of bacteria in a negative light, but just as in our gut, the right bacteria are vital. Bacteria are tiny organisms performing many functions in the soil. They decompose organic matter, some form partnerships with other soil organisms such as legumes, some even suppress disease in plants. They feed, reproduce and excrete, all of which produces a bacterial slime which helps to stick together soil particles, creating good soil structure, allowing air to reach the root zone. Air is an important part of the soil makeup. In soils short of air, such as compacted or waterlogged soils, plants find it much harder to access nutrients. In soils with poor structure, CO_2 produced by organisms in the soil builds up as it can't escape. If this mixes with water it can form a weak acid, acidifying the soil.

Fungi-fruiting bodies on a rotting log of *leylandii*

Fungal hyphae

Most plants in wild or natural settings form beneficial relationships with mycorrhizal fungi. This partnership allows root exudates (fluids) from the plant to be exchanged for nutrients from the fungal hyphae which it obtained from the soil. Fungal hyphae spread over a large area allowing the plant to extend its reach below the soil, accessing nutrients from well beyond the plant's own root zone. Mycorrhizal fungi also help fight off soil pests such as parasitic nematodes, non-beneficial fungi and bacteria.

How to assess soil health at the start

When assessing a site for a new forest garden, nothing is as pleasing as finding a beautiful, dark, crumbly soil to begin with. We are not all that lucky, in fact I rarely come across such wonderful soil. Before you begin, as part of your survey, you should do an assessment of your soil. You could send a sample off to a lab but in all honesty the information you get back is not always very helpful without a soil science degree to interpret it. A more useful way to explore your soil is to dig a few test pits. These don't have to be big; start with one roughly 50 x 50cm and dig down until you hit subsoil; this is usually much paler and should be obvious when you hit it. You can start to make observations such as: is the soil compacted, stony, boggy or sandy? How deep is the topsoil? My garden topsoil was about 4cm at the site of my first ever forest garden patch.

A test pit to explore the soil

Jar test

To measure soil texture and determine the ratios of sand, silt and clay in your soil you can do a simple 'jar test'. Take a handful of soil from just below the surface from each test pit and put it in a large jar. Top the jar up with water, put the lid on and give it a really good shake. Leave it overnight until it settles and the water at the top becomes clear. You should have visible layers that form as different parts of the soil settle at different speeds. Sand is heaviest so will settle out first, the next layer will be silt, then the final layer will be clay particles which may take some time to settle as they are very fine. Organic matter tends to float or settle very slowly. An 'ideal' soil is 40% sand, 40% silt and 20% clay but very few soils will have that exact makeup. Traditionally these tests have been used to decide what amendments need to be added to the soil to change it. A more sustainable approach is to choose plants suited to your soil and just keep adding organic matter in the form of a mulch each year. Organic matter helps sandy soils to retain moisture and helps to break up clay soils improving their drainage.

Worm count

A great indicator of the health of your soil is how many worms there are when you dig your test pit. There should be several worms in each spade full if the soil is healthy. A good rule of thumb is that a hole 30 x 30 x 30cm should have at least 10 worms in. If you find no worms at all, that is an indicator that you have very poor soil. This may be due to compaction, waterlogging or lack of any organic matter and therefore food source. Add a thick mulch of organic matter and the worm population should improve greatly.

pH test

Doing a simple pH test will determine whether your soil is acidic or alkaline. These are available in most garden centres or online. The pH of your soil will determine which plants will thrive in your garden. It really is not worth trying to change the pH of your soil; it is better to go with what you have and choose plants that will grow well in your soil type. If you are desperate to grow plants requiring different conditions to your site you could grow them in containers, but they will not benefit from being connected to the soil food web in the rest of the forest garden soil.

Creating healthy soil

What you add to your soil depends greatly on what you have to begin with. As mentioned before, if soil is very compacted, digging in organic matter before planting can help to create a good soil for the long term. If the soil is not compacted or rubble, I would always choose to add organic matter to the surface instead to improve the soil; this way there is as little disturbance as possible to the soil life already present. In nature soil is created from the top down. Each year vegetation, leaves and dead wood are deposited on the soil surface. In a new garden I put down a layer of well-rotted organic matter before planting, such as manure, homemade compost or leafmould. This way a certain amount will get mixed in as I am planting without any unnecessary disturbance. Once all the plants are in, I mulch with organic matter, ideally ramial woodchip (see below), to suppress the weed seeds from germinating. This mulch layer does not need to be fully composted, in fact it is best to have organic matter at all different stages of decomposition to ensure a range of food to satisfy the diets of a range of soil organisms. Some prefer fresh cut growth and some thrive on already rotting organic matter. If you only add fully rotted mulches, there is nothing for the decomposers to eat. It is tradition in the annual vegetable garden to only use fully rotted compost otherwise you will encourage slugs. Woody twiggy matter is also avoided as it would get dug in when harvesting annuals and affect the nitrogen available to plants. In the perennial forest garden the plants are less prone to slug damage and the non-composted materials are vital food and habitat for the soil organisms and other wildlife.

There is an area in my forest garden where the soil was very poor, like dust. After planting rhubarb, creeping comfrey, giant fleabane (*Inula magnifica*) and *Trachystemon* the soil has come alive with a lovely crumbly texture, staying moist in the driest of summers. The soil food web develops and thrives in symbiosis with the plants growing in your forest garden so the mere act of planting up your garden with a diverse range of plants will begin the process of improving your soil. As the plant roots grow, die back and rot down, they will constantly add organic matter deep down in the soil without the need for any digging. In this way all plants are dynamic accumulators, cycling nutrients as they add organic matter to the soil.

I dug under a pile of rotting grass and the soil was full of worms

How to maintain soil health

The best way to maintain a thriving soil food web is to only use natural fertilisers made from organic material such as compost, manure, straw etc. Soil dwellers such as worms, springtails and bacteria are repelled or killed by synthetic fertilisers, destroying the soil food web. This means the loss of all the important roles these creatures play in building soil and making nutrients available to plants. Weedkillers and fungicides kill mycorrhizal fungi, destroying their network that provides nutrients to the plants and fights off infections. Once the source of nutrients from the soil food web has been destroyed, plants are dependent on a constant supply of synthetic fertilisers, requiring applications throughout the year. This creates work for us and puts the health of our plants and the whole ecosystem of the forest garden at risk, not to mention the wider environmental damage. Natural fertilisers in the form of organic matter are broken down slowly by the soil life so are naturally slow release, meaning an annual application is all that is required to keep the soil life well fed.

Ramial woodchip

Ramial woodchips are amazing! There is a huge difference between ramial woodchip and the chipped bark found in bags in the garden centre. Bark bought in bags in garden centres is just that, pure bark and almost always from softwood coniferous trees. Softwoods contain high levels of tannins which actually suppress the growth of deciduous plants. The addition of this chipped bark to the surface will encourage soil fungi and bacteria who benefit conifers, whereas our plants will mostly be deciduous and non-coniferous. If the origin of our woodchips is from deciduous branches, then adding them to the surface will encourage the right types of soil organisms to suit our plants.

Ramial woodchips are made from branches/trunks that have a diameter of 7cm or less and from deciduous species of tree or shrub. This is important because as the diameter of a branch increases, so does the nitrogen/carbon ratio, meaning woodchip from thicker branches containing a higher ratio of carbon is harder for soil organisms to break down and contains less nutrients. Ramial woodchips provide a brilliant long-term food source for decomposers in

Chipping thin branches to make ramial woodchip using an electric chipper

▲ Mulching the forest garden with ramial woodchip

▶ Laying down cardboard before adding the mulch to stop weeds growing back in a newly planted area

➡ Cut grass can be used as a mulch where it won't be in direct contact with stems or leaves. This mulberry is in very shallow soil and needed a boost; an upside down plastic pot with the bottom cut out and a slit down the side helped to prevent the fresh grass causing rot on the trunk.

the soil, a real feast. When I have mulched with ramial woodchips I soon find a very visible network of fine white mycorrhizal fungi hyphae have developed. Within 12 months the soil beneath it has a noticeable increase in the amount of worms and has become more friable. A clear indication of an increase in healthy soil life.

It can be hard to gather enough suitable material from a small garden so it is worth contacting friends and neighbours to see if anyone wants their hedge trimming or any trees or shrubs cutting back. These can then be chipped in a small electric chipper, which are relatively inexpensive to buy or can be hired. If you can only make a small amount of chipped wood, spread it on a different patch each year in a layer around 5cm deep, rather than spreading it very thinly. This is because the layer needs to be thick enough to provide the right conditions for the fungi. You can rotate which areas get ramial woodchips and which get a different mulch each year. If it is impossible to

find a source it isn't a disaster; there are many other types of mulch that will do a great job to help your forest garden thrive, but if you can find a way to add some kind of wood, even just in the form of twigs and sticks, to the surface of your garden each year, you will really help develop a diverse soil ecology.

Leafmould also makes an excellent mulch; it is nature's mulch as each year the leaves fall from the trees where they rot down or are pulled down by worms. There are several ways to make leafmould to use as a mulch. You can simply make a pile in an unused corner of the garden, make a container out of chicken wire or slatted wood if you want something neater or even just bin liners or old compost bags tied at the top but make sure there are plenty of holes in the sides to let the air in so the decomposition process can occur. If you were going to use leafmould as part of soil improvement to be dug in, then you would need to leave the leaves for a minimum of two years to ensure they were fully composted.

If you are spreading them as mulch, one year is fine as once spread over the ground, you will be providing a food source for the soil life on the surface. You can use freshly collected leaves but they can blow about, collecting in piles which can get quite deep in places and exclude light to plants you want to grow.

Whatever you decide to mulch your garden with, the ideal is to have acquired it locally from a sustainable source without causing damage to the area you collected it from. If that is from within your own garden that is great. If this is not possible then ask friends, neighbours, local allotment holders or even the local council if you can gather materials from their property such as leaves, branches or composting materials. It is important to check no herbicides or pesticides have been used on the area you are collecting from as these may persist in the vegetation; causing damage to rather than feeding your soil life. This is also the case for leaves gathered from roadsides where fuel or other pollutants may accumulate.

Liquid feeds and compost teas

It may seem to contradict all the traditional garden teaching to feed the soil rather than the plants but the effect of synthetic feeds watered or sprinkled on the soil is actually very destructive to your garden. The soil food web cannot thrive due to the inhospitable conditions meaning organic matter doesn't get broken down efficiently, soil structure is ruined and the plants become totally dependent on their next synthetic fix to stay alive. The plants may look green and lush but they are certainly not the sign of a healthy garden. The addition of nitrogen fixing and nutrient accumulating plants to our forest gardens, along with an annual mulch, is all that is required to keep your garden fertilised and your soil food web thriving.

On a smaller scale, forest gardens often include some containerised plants such as in a living green wall or pots where the garden is paved. You may have included hungry annuals in your forest garden beds that will need something to top up nutrient

Comfrey 'Hidcote Blue' flowers are great for bees and the leaves can be cut for making compost tea or liquid feed

levels, especially in the containers where the same nutrient cycling cannot easily be achieved. Where I need to do supplementary feeding I make my own liquid feed. Fill a container, such as a bucket, with freshly cut leaves of your chosen plant, then fill with water and wait for a couple of weeks. Be warned it will get very smelly. Strain out the sludge then dilute this liquid down further, to roughly 1 part liquid to 10 parts water. It's not an exact science. Different plants can be used to make the feed depending on what nutrients you want to add. By using cut comfrey leaves you can create a feed high in potassium which is good for fruiting plants: nettle leaves make a feed high in nitrogen which is great for leafy growth. Mix together for something a bit more balanced.

If a plant is starting to turn a paler green or even yellow, that is a good indicator of nitrogen deficiency; the nettle feed would help give the plant a boost. Yellowing between the leaf veins and brown edges, almost like they have been burnt, is a sign of potassium deficiency; the comfrey feed should help remedy this. Leaves turning bronze, purple or brown is often an indicator of phosphorous deficiency; additions of bone meal can add phosphorus to the soil. These are the three main nutrients needed for

plants to thrive although there are many others vital for plant growth. Your perennial plants in the ground should not need this liquid feed if you are managing to give them plenty of organic mulch each year which will contain many nutrients but if you are harvesting something heavily, such as chives or a perennial kale, or you have hungry annuals in your polyculture, they may benefit from some liquid feeding.

If you want a feed that will store, especially useful if you want a feed early in the spring before nettles and comfrey have grown big enough to get a decent harvest, or you want to avoid a stinking bucket of vegetation in your garden every few weeks, you can extract the juices from leaves. At Growing with Grace in Clapham I have seen them use a pipe that they stuff full of comfrey or nettles and then add a weight to squash the leaves through the pipe. At the bottom of the pipe is a funnel filled with gravel and sand to filter out the rotting vegetation. The leaves break down as the weight squashes them and the juices drip out of the bottom into a bottle to be stored for later use. Simple technology. You could use a bucket or water butt with a tap at the bottom, or a container with a hole in, with a funnel underneath. This will be a much stronger solution than the liquid feed made

Nitrogen fixing plants

Tree layer	Alder (*Alnus* sp.)	Coppice every few years to keep small.
Shrub layer	Broom (*Cytisus* sp.)	Grows well on poor soils and can be used in basketry or to make brooms and brushes.
	Elaeagnus sp.	There are many species to choose from, some with tasty berries.
	Sea buckthorn (*Hippophae rhamnoides*)	It has delicious zesty berries but it can cause problems as it suckers and spreads.
	Gorse (*Ulex europaeus*)	Another plant that does well on poor soils. Beware as it is very prickly but that quality makes it great as a defensive hedge.
Herbaceous layer	*Lupinus* sp.	There are both annual and perennial lupins, some with edible seeds.
Groundcover layer	Clover (*Trifolium* sp.)	The annual clovers are very pretty but can be quite vigorous. There are some very attractive small *Trifolium repens* which are perennial and creep across the ground.
Rhizome layer	Groundnuts (*Apios americana*)	This could also be in the climbers category due to its long vines.
	Earthnut pea (*Lathyrus tuberosus*)	This climbing pea also has edible tubers.
Climbers	Peas (*Lathyrus* sp.)	Mostly annuals but there is a perennial pea which has attractive flowers.
	Beans (*Phaseolus* sp.)	There are many types of beans from huge climbers many metres high to small bush beans which would fit better in the herbaceous layer.

with water so will need diluting more. Usually it's a case of trying to make it 'weak tea' coloured. Try 1 part liquid feed to 15 or 20 parts water.

I would also like to make a wee argument for using urine. It is a fantastic balanced liquid fertiliser containing, amongst others, a very balanced mix of the three main nutrients: nitrogen, potassium and phosphorus. It is a free resource so fits well in a permaculture garden. It is safe to use so long as you don't take any medications or have a urine infection. We use it diluted 1 part urine to 10 parts water in containers. It is best used on perennial or fruiting plants rather than directly on leafy annuals you will be eating. During the summer we feed our hungry pumpkins in the yard forest garden weekly with diluted urine on 'wee wee Wednesdays' so we always remember to feed them on the same day, once a week.

These raspberries are not looking very happy so I will give them a good mulch of homemade compost and in the spring a few feeds of comfrey liquid fertiliser if they've still not improved

Making compost

Making your own homemade compost doesn't have to be complicated. If you send all green waste to the tip you are losing fertility from the system. By incorporating a composting system into your design you can catch and store the energy that was leaving your system and return it in the form of a mulch. Organic matter from the house can be used as a fresh mulch directly onto the garden but it can attract slugs and rats: better to compost it a bit first. Your compost heap can be a simple pile or you can enclose it with sides if space is limited or even use the plastic tower type. Build it straight onto the soil so that any organisms already in the soil such as worms can get access. There are whole books on compost making but the most important thing to remember is to get a reasonable balance of 'green' materials such as grass clippings, fresh cut foliage, kitchen vegetable scraps etc. and 'brown' materials such as card, paper, straw, leaves etc. If grass clippings and vegetable scraps are your main outputs from the house and garden, keep adding some dry leaves stored from winter or ripped up card or shredded paper to help soak up the moisture and keep the compost pile active and balanced.

I like to add some branchy twiggy bits in too to help create air pockets to keep it aerated without the need to turn it. It doesn't matter if these woody bits haven't broken down fully as I will be adding them to the surface rather than digging them in. Nitrogen robbery happens when you dig carbon-rich woody material into the soil. In order for the organisms in the soil to break them down, they use nitrogen already in the soil meaning there is much less available for the plants. When you add this same woody material to the surface of the soil instead, it only robs nitrogen from the very surface bit of soil. As it breaks down on the surface, nutrients are slowly released into the soil whilst the soil life gets a massive boost from the new food source applied as occurs in nature, in layers to the soil surface.

Plastic compost bins can be useful in small gardens. If you have two, you can be filling one while the other is rotting down.

In summary, to keep your forest garden plants healthy you need to feed your soil with organic matter; the soil food web will then take care of your plants; nutritional needs. If you remove the plants' dead leaves and stems in the autumn, apply organic matter in a layer to the surface during the autumn/winter. Alternatively you can 'chop and drop' and add some additional organic matter to replace the nutrients lost by harvesting. Adding nitrogen fixing and nutrient accumulating plants to your design can help your forest garden meet its own nutritional needs but it can be a challenge in small gardens to get the balance right. You will probably want a higher ratio of edible to nutrient accumulating plants than a larger scale forest garden.

Collecting seed of
Smyrnium perfoliatum

CHAPTER 8

How to Propagate Your Forest Garden

When we began our first forest garden, the garden was prepared and plans were drawn up, yet we had a very small budget for buying plants. Fortunately, Andrew and I are trained horticulturalists who have a real passion for propagation, very useful skills to get the ball rolling on the cheap. The temptation is to buy as large and mature a plant as you can afford. We took a different approach, following the permaculture principle 'small and slow solutions'. It is well documented that relatively mature containerised specimens perform poorly compared to their younger and bare root counterparts. Young tree whips (one-year-old seedlings) are much less prone to transplant shock and in a relatively short space of time will outgrow more expensive nursery specimens with their cramped roots and often poor growing medium. We have a few living reminders in our larger forest garden area where, more than a decade later, small shrubs are not much bigger than the day we planted them. If I dug them out I would probably find the roots in a knotted tangled mess. Root systems on the bare-root trees and shrubs will be stronger and more often than not, won't require staking.

I often see forest gardens that have been planted too densely, with a gradual shading out of the lower layers. When you have spent up to £40 on a fruit tree it takes a lot of courage to remove it. If however you have grafted your own tree at a cost of around £3, you are more ready to thin it out if it is in the way later on. This way you can get 10-plus trees for the price of one. It also allows you to assess what grows well in the microclimate that is your garden, removing anything that is not fruiting well, is struggling with pest or disease attack, or with hindsight, was in the wrong place to start with. Many people panic at the thought of propagation as if it requires you to be born with 'green fingers', but with patience and experimentation, propagation can be really fun. You get a real glow of satisfaction when you plant up a garden with plants you have grown yourself from seed or cuttings and it satisfies my Yorkshire inclination to save money wherever possible.

Andrew grafted this crab apple he named 'Pink Juice' from a self-seeded tree we found on a walk

◄ Labelling the seedling nut trees in the nursery beds

▲ Seed of *Smyrnium perfoliatum*

Propagation techniques

Seed saving and sowing

I always carry bags in my pocket in case we happen to come across an interesting plant, ripe with seeds, just crying out to be taken home. This may be from a wild rose bush with unusually large and fleshy fruits or some escapee garden lupin, growing happily in a grassy verge that may do well in my meadow and fix nitrogen for the edible crops. Always ask permission from the landowner before collecting fruit or small cuttings. Many popular forest garden plants can be grown from seed, tubers or bulbs, with the list of suppliers growing ever larger. Even eBay has been quite a treasure trove for seed with a few online shops specialising in edible perennials.

We sow seed in seed trays or modules but you can improvise with toilet roll inserts or plastic food trays, such as those you can buy mushrooms in; just don't forget to punch some holes in the bottom for drainage. If the seed came with instructions, follow them. Certain seed, especially of trees and shrubs, has very specific requirements, such as a period of cold before it will germinate, without which it will sit and rot (this is called stratification). Other seed will germinate easily; it is very specific to each plant. If you have foraged seed it is worth taking the time to research its germination requirements which are usually available online.

Seed sowing

Ideally a seed compost is used to give ideal conditions, such as good drainage and aeration for most seeds to germinate and grow on to small seedlings. You can use multi-purpose compost but ideally you would sieve it to separate out any large chunks that may impede germination. Pile your compost into your seed tray/repurposed container, give it a little shake from side to side to make sure it is distributed evenly over the whole area, then gently press it down with your fingers or the bottom of a pot, but without compacting it. If any compost is above the edge of the tray, use a piece of wood to take off the excess by running it along the top of the container in a sort of sawing action. Sow the seeds by sprinkling evenly over the whole area then cover by sieving a fine layer until the seeds are just covered. The depth of compost to cover the seed depends on the size of the seed. A general rule of thumb is to cover them with a depth equal to their own thickness. Don't forget to label them, ideally with a reused plastic label or a strip of plastic milk bottle, with the name written in pencil or permanent marker. I have tried wooden lolly sticks but for perennials which may take a while to germinate I found the wood had gone black and I could no longer read the writing. Water carefully to avoid washing the seeds into ridges in the trays. You can use a fine rose on a watering can or sit the tray in a container of water until the surface is moist, soaking up the water from below like a sponge. You can water seed trays with a spray bottle or you can even get tiny roses that screw onto average sized water bottles if you don't have the space to store a watering can.

Pricking out

Keep the compost moist but not so wet it causes rotting. Eventually the seeds should germinate. The time until this happens depends a lot on what you are growing. Some may take days, some years, so it is worth finding out how long it should take so you can keep an eye out. Once the seedlings are big enough to handle they can be pricked out; this means transferred from the seed tray into larger pots for growing on. If left in the seed trays the seedlings would soon be in competition with each other and run out of nutrients, which stunts growth. If you have a lot of seedlings, select the healthiest from those that have germinated. I love this stage as seedlings are not genetically identical to the parent plant, as with taking cuttings. I enjoy imagining how these new plants will differ from their parents, hopefully larger and tastier fruits or sweeter, more tender leaves. Growing from seed has mixed blessings as you can just as easily end up with smaller, blander fruits or more bitter leaves, but you get the added advantage of increased genetic diversity which brings added resilience to our systems.

Use a small dibber or pencil to separate and lift the seedling out of the tray whilst holding the seedling very gently by the leaves with the other hand, avoiding crushing the stems. Use the same dibber to make a hole in a pot of compost and lower the roots into the hole. Firm the soil around the roots with the dibber then water immediately. Where you grow these will depend on what you are growing. The seedling may need the greenhouse or cold frame if tender; details should be on the seed packet. Once perennials have grown on for a year they should be ready to plant out; if they are a tree or shrub seedling they may need another year. Annuals would need to be planted as soon as they are big enough to compete with the other plants in your forest garden.

We also direct sow some seed either straight into the forest garden if there is a bare patch of soil, or in a dedicated seed bed. This is a raised bed for germinating seedlings and growing them on until they are big enough to be transplanted. I made our seed beds with four pieces of pallet wood joined at the corners and placed onto the ground over several sheets of cardboard to kill off any existing vegetation. I filled the bed with a mixture of compost, leafmould and some horticultural sand. You can just use pure compost but the sand increases drainage to reduce rotting and fungal disease. You can then sow your seeds directly into the bed in rows. Label well as some shrub

Seedlings of cosmos planted out into the forest garden with plenty of space to grow

and tree seeds can take a year or two to germinate.

I love to sprinkle foxglove seeds around the garden and see where they pop up: I think they look beautiful wherever they emerge. Developing your seedling identification skills is really useful; you can take out seedlings you don't want at an early stage and leave those you do want to spread about without removing them by accident. It's all about careful and regular observation.

More often than not you end up with way more seedlings than you need. This is a great opportunity to share or swap with others rather than all that effort going to waste on the compost heap. Perhaps someone down the road has loads of saltbush cuttings going spare but is wanting a few plants of the Caucasion spinach (*Hablitzia*) you have just potted up. Keep an eye out for seed swaps in your area or online. If you can't find one then maybe think about organising one. Seeds can be expensive but there may be someone nearby who has the plant you need and wouldn't mind if you collected a few seeds. Collect seeds when they are ripe and dry them somewhere dry but not hot, either in a paper or organza (sheer fabric) bag. Once you are sure they are dry, store them in an airtight container, such as a jar or sealed plastic bag, somewhere cool until you are ready to sow. If the seeds are fleshy you can remove the flesh by fermenting them for a week or so in a jar of water then rinsing them. The seeds should sink and you can remove the flesh as it floats to the top. If some flesh remains it won't matter so long as you dry it all thoroughly before storing.

The walking onion develops bulbils instead of seed. As the head falls to the ground, the bulbils develop roots and grow a new plant. These can be potted up.

Pea seeds are sown directly in the ground to climb over the willow arch

Cuttings

From early winter until spring you can take cuttings of many shrubs and fruit bushes. Currants and gooseberries in particular are very easy to grow from cuttings. When propagating our shrub layer we took cuttings of blackcurrants, redcurrants and gooseberries by taking sections roughly 30cm long of the newest wood (this year's growth) that is at least pencil thickness. These were pushed into the ground through a hole in a cardboard layer used to exclude weeds and keep moisture in. Push them in until only two or three buds are above the ground, roughly 5cm, then leave for a year, only watering in very dry weather. In 12 months' time the cuttings should have developed a good root system and then can be transplanted to their final position. You can also put them into tall pots instead of the ground if you don't have a suitable space in the ground. I prefer to 'strike' them directly into the ground so I don't need to keep watering them. I have a small bed roughly 1m square for growing on cuttings.

The same principle applies to many shrubs including weaving materials such as dogwoods and willow. You can also 'strike' these cuttings directly into their final positions if there won't be competition from other plants until they establish. There are many other exciting ways of propagating from existing trees and shrubs, such as softwood cuttings, layering and air layering. I heartily recommend having a go. It's very satisfying to create your own new plant. A great book with some very useful illustrations is *RHS Plant Propagation* by Philip McMillan Browse.

Adventitious roots on this gooseberry stem mean it can be snipped off and potted up to form a new plant

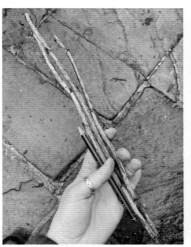

▲ Hardwood cuttings need to be pencil thickness or more

▶ Taking cuttings from established fruit bushes

⏩ Striking hardwood cuttings in nursery beds

Grafting

In our garden we graft all our own trees, from Yorkshire apples to Serbian quince. Grafting is where you join two parts of different plants together to make one plant. The scion is the top part from the plant you want to grow and the rootstock is the rooting part, which is used to control the size, vigour and sometimes disease resistance of the tree or shrub. There are many different grafting techniques and it would be impossible to cover all of these here so if you fancy giving it a go, look out for courses near you; they are becoming more and more available. There are some good step-by-step tutorials online and many books on the subject, my favourite being *The Grafter's Handbook* by R.J. Garner. Give it a go and if it isn't successful, you can grow the rootstock on for a year and try again. In early spring we use 'whip and tongue' grafting for apples, pears, quince, medlar and even plums and cherries, budding is often used for cherries and plums. We collect scion wood cuttings (the part from the cultivar you want to grow) in the coldest winter months when the plant is dormant and wrap them up well in a plastic bag to prevent them drying out. We keep these 15-20cm long, pencil thick scions dormant in the fridge, ready to graft in February or March, once the sap has begun to rise in the rootstocks.

Ideally the rootstock stem will match the thickness of the scionwood you have, as when you join them together you want as much of the cambium layer as possible to be in contact; this is the actively growing tissues just below the bark layer. When making your cut you also want to work quickly to make a clean cut and join the two pieces together before the tissues dry out and die off. Make a diagonal cut along and through the scion wood about 4cm long; this gives a much bigger surface area for the cambium layers to join than a straight across cut. Slice the 'tongue' about 1cm long, about one third of the way down the cut.

(Whip grafting is one diagonal cut without the tongue.) Make a corresponding diagonal cut on the rootstock about 20-25cm above soil level with a corresponding slice one third of the way up the cut. This tongue helps to stabilise the graft union until it has healed. Line up the cambium layers as best you can so that at least one side lines up exactly. I use an elastic band cut into a strip to hold the graft into position then wrap it in polythene tape to prevent the tissues from drying out. You can soon tell if it has taken as the buds of the scion wood will burst and grow. If the top part continues to do well, the polythene tape can be removed in the autumn as the tissues should have made a join strong enough to hold the two parts together.

Autumn foraging trips offer an ideal opportunity to discover unique wild trees, grown from the seed of cultivated fruit tossed into a verge or wild area. We have created several tasty apple trees and a pear tree this way, collecting the scion wood in winter and grafting them to plant at home, excited to put them through their paces on our site. Our favourite is one we have called 'Morrisons'; it was a wild tree growing in a roadside hedgerow close to the supermarket near Andrew's parents' house. We foraged from it many times and I am glad we grafted it because a few years ago it was bulldozed away for a new housing estate.

To reduce the height of our canopy layer we have chosen appropriate dwarfing rootstocks. For our apples we are using MM106; M26 is more dwarfing and would give us smaller trees but we have poor soil on a north-west facing slope so we need a bit more vigour. We have also had success with grafting pear onto hawthorn, a tree that grows well here. The long-term success and overall size of these trees on hawthorn is pretty unknown but I love a good experiment and if they become unruly they will make fragrant firewood.

Whip and tongue grafting

Foraging for apples

Dwarfing rootstocks

Apple	M27	Extremely dwarfing	1.2-1.8m x 1.5m
	M9	Dwarfing	1.8-2.4m x 2.7m
	M26	Dwarfing	2.4-3m x 3.6m
Pears and Quinces	Quince C	Dwarfing	2.5-3m
Plums and Gages	Pixy	Semi-dwarfing	3-4m
Plums, Gages, Damsons, Apricots, Nectarines, Peaches	St Julian A	Semi-vigorous	4.5-5m
	Torinel	Semi-vigorous	2.4-3m
Cherry	Gisela 5	Semi-dwarfing	2.4-3m

▲ Dividing a clump of *Viola* 'Freckles'
with two hand forks

▼ Pulling the divisions apart into
smaller pieces ready to pot up

Divisions

Divisions are by far the easiest way to propagate hardy herbaceous perennials as they don't require the time or attention of seedlings. Be resourceful and ask friends, neighbours or even perfect strangers for a clump or two of a useful perennial they may have in abundance when spotted over a garden wall. You could always exchange it for something you have in abundance. Pieces taken from around the edges (the most productive part) will be actively growing and perform best. Alternatively you can buy one plant, pamper it with plenty of room, making sure it doesn't get hungry or thirsty and in no time at all you will be amazed how many plants you can get for your small investment by lifting and dividing it in the autumn.

Using a bow saw to chop up agapanthus as the root ball is too dense to pull apart

This *Primula denticulata* is spreading out nicely after planting it as a tiny division the previous spring

I love to dig plants up to investigate their roots. Dividing some, such as *Primula*, is easy as the plant almost falls apart into many little individual plants, or can easily be separated by inserting two hand forks back to back and pushing the handles together. Others are more tricky with brittle or tough roots creating a tangle too dense to tease apart. If you have a big clump that is proving impossible to divide, you can slice it into pieces with a sharp spade. If it is a smaller plant, I prefer to get out my pen knife or even saw to slice the plant into chunks. It may seem brutal but so long as you have some roots attached to a bit of crown (the above ground growing point), the piece should grow into a new plant. You can replant these chunks directly into the garden or pot up to give away or swap.

Propagating is my passion; I only visit garden centres for the odd rarity, to window shop or for a nice slice of cake. My advice would be to invest in a good propagation guide and ask someone who knows their stuff to show you how. If you don't know anyone, look for a course; it will give you the confidence to give it a go and in the long run will save you money. You might just get hooked like us and start dreaming up plans to create a community forest garden to use up all your spare plants.

Ajuga reptans, Nepalese raspberry (*Rubus nepalensis*) and globe artichoke make a lovely combination in shades of purple

CHAPTER 9

Plant Profiles

want to share my love of plants with everyone, whilst understanding we all have individual tastes and needs. I have included information about a select few plants with some details of my experience of growing them. There are thousands of plants you could choose and I don't feel it necessary to list them all, so I have chosen just a few of my favourites for suitability in a small-scale forest garden. This list should be used for inspiration rather than something rigid to copy. Experimentation is an important part of being a gardener and each garden has different microclimates and each forest gardener has their own individual needs. Think of this list as a handy starting point. Unlike some of the more obscure perennial edibles, most of these plants will give a decent yield and are palatable to the average person. I would encourage you to seek out and taste as many as you can before making your final selection; this should ensure your forest garden is full of plants you actually want to eat rather than one full of technically edible plants that you never harvest. My go-to resource for edible and useful plants is the Plants for a Future database and book, which includes a fantastic detailed catalogue of plants suitable for the UK climate.

I have listed plants by layer within the forest garden. The upper and lower canopy trees overlap in a small garden as you don't have space for the typical upper canopy species such as walnut or sweet chestnut. Two layers can be achieved where there is space by growing semi-dwarfing or small trees for the upper layer and dwarf fruit trees for the lower canopy.

This whole small-scale forest garden was propagated by ourselves using seed, cuttings, grafting and divisions

Upper and lower canopy trees

Apple 'McIntosh' growing in a forest garden patch

Pear 'Durondeau' ready for harvesting. Photo: Neil Chapman

Apples

There are so many varieties to choose from and if you only have room for one or two trees, that decision is even more important. When whittling down your choices, consider the size you require and select the appropriate rootstock. Look at disease resistance, such as for mildew and canker, and lastly think about flavour. I have found, to my peril, that going with flavour first can mean having to cut down and burn a tree that is prone to disease: a waste of time and money and utterly heartbreaking. There are many apple days all over the country each autumn where you can taste apples to get an idea of what you like.

If you would like more than one variety of apple in a tiny space you can graft a 'family tree' where two or more varieties are grafted onto the same one rootstock. This can help with pollination too if the varieties flower at the same time and can pollinate each other.

Propagation. You can grow apples from seed but they may take many years to fruit and qualities such as size, flavour and disease resistance are totally unknown because they don't come true to the parent tree. This is fine if you have acres to spare and can experiment, but not great if you can only fit

one tree in your garden. Grafting is explained in the chapter on propagation.

Maintenance. Prune if necessary to remove dead or dying wood and to keep to size if needed. Mulch each year with woodchip or similar such as homemade compost.

Pear

There is much less choice when it comes to pears, especially if you are in a cold climate. I grow a delicious variety called 'Durondeau' against a south facing wall in West Yorkshire; and 'Beth' has also done well here. Ask around at local allotments, community gardens and nurseries to find out which varieties grow well in your area.

Maintenance. As for apple.

Cherry
(*Prunus avium* and *Prunus cerasus*)

I love homegrown cherries but I often find the birds steal them all before they are ripe enough for us to enjoy. For this reason, think carefully before choosing a cherry if it is to be the only tree in your forest garden. Netting trees at harvest time can trap and kill birds by accident so not an ideal solution. We grow a yellow variety called 'Donissens Gold' which we have found to confuse the birds as they think the fruit is not yet ripe and leave them alone.

Propagation. Cherries are usually grafted as they don't come true from seed. If grown from seed, the eventual size of the tree will be unknown and it may be many years before you get fruit to decide if it has a nice flavour, so I would always recommend grafted trees for small gardens where obtaining a good yield from each tree is important.

Maintenance. As with other fruit trees, prune out the dead, diseased and dying growth. Sweet cherries, *Prunus avium*, should be pruned in late summer as they are very susceptible to bacterial canker and silver leaf which are more likely to infect exposed cuts in winter. Morello or acid cherries, *Prunus cerasus*, are more shade tolerant than sweet cherries. They also differ in that they produce their fruit on the previous season's wood, so more care needs to be taken when pruning to ensure you don't prune off the productive part of the branch. In late summer, prune back about a quarter of the shoots that have fruited, back to a healthy younger side shoot which will produce the fruit in the following year.

Plum, gage, damson (*Prunus domestica* ssp.) and mirabelle (*Prunus cerasifera*)

I was never a fan of plums when I was younger but I have grown to love them. There is nothing quite like a freshly picked juicy plum, straight from the tree and still warm from the sun. Mirabelles are a small golden cherry plum. Mirabelle and elderflower jam was our bestseller when we had our market stall. We foraged for them just off the Pennine Way. In my northerly north-west facing garden I struggle to grow many plums other than 'Marjorie's Seedling' due to late frosts damaging the flowers, but when we get a crop it is well worth it.

Plums and gages need more sheltered spots than damsons and have a much sweeter flavour. Damsons

Blossom of mirabelle planted as part of a hedge alongside alder, perennial kale and raspberries

are used for cooking with the addition of something sweet like sugar to make them more palatable. 'Marjorie's Seedling', which is a dual purpose plum for cooking and eating fresh, is also self-fertile so won't need another plum to pollinate it but will probably produce a higher yield if it has a pollinator. This has been our most reliable cropper.

Propagation. Grafting is the usual method as plants do not come true from seed.

Maintenance. As with the cherries and other stone fruits, trees are pruned in summer to reduce the risk of infection from silver leaf or bacterial canker. Start by taking out the dead, diseased and dying growth. Don't take out too much growth at once as this will reduce the vigour of the tree. If you want to reduce the size of the tree, do this over three years by removing one third of the biggest branches each year in late summer.

Cornelian cherry (*Cornus mas*)

This beautiful small tree, growing to around 5-10m, is a heavenly sight on a sunny winter's day. It looks like it is glowing as the tiny star-like yellow flowers appear in February/March time, before the leaves have appeared. This early flowering tree, which can be pruned as a shrub, is valuable forage for bees. Small edible red oblong fruits around 2cm long are produced, ripening in late summer. The berries can have quite an acidic taste when eaten raw and need to be fully ripe. They can be made into a sauce similar to cranberry sauce.

Propagation. You can grow it from seed, ideally fresh seed with the flesh removed (this contains germination inhibitors) but it can be slow to germinate and takes many years to bear fruit. Plants grown from cuttings will bear fruit much sooner. Semi-ripe cuttings can be taken in late summer/autumn from this season's growth or you can layer the branches. I have grown 'Jolico' which has larger fruits but, if I'm honest, it's a struggle to get them before the birds do; I am happy to share some of my crop in exchange for some valuable pest control.

Maintenance. Minimal other than mulching and occasional pruning back of shoots that are growing where you don't want them.

Hazel (*Corylus avellana*) and filbert (*Corylus maxima*)

I don't really grow hazels or filberts for nuts as the squirrels usually take them before they are fully ripe but they are valuable plants for harvesting poles. By removing one third of the stems each year, I have a constant supply of poles for using around the garden

Hazel coppice managed to produce long straight poles for use in the garden

for plant labels, bean poles, fencing and basketry, and I like to carve a spoon or two from the thicker base of the stems. Because you are removing the largest branches each year it keeps the tree small and manageable for smaller forest gardens. You can coppice the whole plant to the ground every five or six years; this is the more traditional way to manage them in a woodland setting but this can be challenging because every time you coppice, you are totally changing the conditions for the other plants around the hazel and the other trees can get quite big in that time, possibly shading out everything else in your forest garden. I love the look of the large leaves; hazel just gives an instant 'feel' of lush woodland.

Propagation. Sow the seed fresh in a seed bed. If using stored seed, soak for 48 hours then give two weeks somewhere warm followed by three months of cold stratification. An easier alternative for hazel is layering or you can often dig up a sucker from the base of the plant in winter, with roots attached, and plant this straight out. These *Corylus* tolerate most soils except very acidic soils and are pretty wind tolerant.

Maintenance. Prune as described above, according to the desired size, thickness and maturity of poles required. A simple mulch of ramial woodchip or leaves is enough.

Alder (*Alnus glutinosa*)

This can be a huge tree but as with the hazel, if you manage it by pruning out one third of the branches each year, they can be kept at a manageable size. Alder is excellent as a windbreak, with the added bonus that bacteria on its roots fix nitrogen from the atmosphere. Every time you prune it back, a boost of nitrogen will be released to the surrounding plants as the roots die back. On our windy hillside we planted alders on the north side of the less wind tolerant fruit such as the apples. This protects them from the cold winter northerly winds, provides nitrogen but crucially doesn't cast any shade. I love to watch out for the distinctive purple buds in winter and wait for the catkins.

It is a very pretty tree in a winter garden. It tolerates soils that are waterlogged in winter but will also grow in drier soils. It tolerates poor infertile soils as it is a pioneer species, often dying out in woodlands once other trees get established. It is an important food source for many caterpillars of butterflies and moths, in turn providing food for birds.

Propagation. Seed can be sown fresh in a seed bed and germinates easily. Seedlings grow quickly so pot them up into two or three-litre pots once they are big enough to handle or they will quickly get congested roots. Hardwood cuttings can be taken of ripe wood in the autumn.

Maintenance. As for hazel.

Pepper tree (*Zanthoxylum schinifolium*)

There are several species of *Zanthoxylum*, each with different flavoured peppercorns and leaves. Nepalese pepper tree is *Zanthoxylum planispinum* with zesty lemony flavoured peppercorns and leaves; it is from the same plant family as lemon and grows to a height of around 3.5-4m. *Zanthoxylum schinifolium*, also known as Szechuan pepper, is another of the smaller pepper trees with more divided leaves. Both trees have large spikes on their branches so care is needed when harvesting. The tree has a long harvesting period as the young leaves can be eaten in small amounts and the peppercorns can be eaten when green by adding to pickles or sauces. Peppercorns ripen in October as they start to split and release the seed. It is the casing that gives the flavour but the seed does not need to be separated. Leave them for a couple of days to dry out then store in an airtight container; they can then be used in a pepper mill. The plants are either male or female so you will need one of each to pollinate the flowers on the female tree.

Propagation. They are easy to grow from seed. Sow in autumn outside to allow cold weather treatment to stimulate germination in spring. If using stored

The purple catkins of alder appear in winter

seed, give some cold treatment in the fridge for a few weeks in a bag with some damp compost. Semi-ripe cuttings can be taken in July to September. Pot up and keep compost moist. Protect over winter for the first two winters, after which the plants are very hardy.

Maintenance. The trees are very easy to look after, simply requiring a mulch each year. You can remove lower branches to allow other lower canopy shrubs and perennials to be planted underneath. If you want to keep them small, they respond well to pruning in spring.

Shrub layer

Rosemary

Previously known as *Rosmarinus officinalis* but now reclassified as *Salvia rosmarinus*.

I use rosemary a lot in cooking but being a Mediterranean herb it is not suited to a woodland setting. I plant rosemary in the sunniest spot I can, in fact I tend to have two or three bushes in the garden because they can rot or be severely damaged by frost in our damp, cold winters in the north of England. Having three makes the supply more resilient, especially if I have a few different varieties. My favourite is 'Green Ginger' but this is one of the more tender varieties and I lost it while it was over-wintering in the unheated greenhouse. There are many different varieties meaning you can try a few out in different situations and for different functions. Upright plants such as 'Tuscan Blue' are good to use the vertical space without smothering too much out and at the opposite end are groundcover varieties, the Prostratus Group, such as 'Capri' with a height of just 15cm which can scramble over rocks or over paving at the edge of a bed.

Propagation. Rosemary can be grown from seed but slow germination means they often rot. It is however very easy to grow from cuttings. In late summer, take semi-ripe cuttings, ideally with a heel, around 5-10cm long, they should root easily, or in spring take softwood cuttings.

Sage (*Salvia officinalis*)

Sage is a hardy evergreen shrub which I love to grow but is short lived in my yard. I have seen some mature specimens in sunnier gardens but they don't like wet winters. If, like me, you have a garden which is in total shade in the winter or you have heavy, damp soil, you could grow sage in a container. They are best grown on the edge of a bed as they don't like competition from other plants stealing their sunlight. They are happy enough with short ground covers underneath such as *Ajuga reptans* or wild strawberries. There are some very ornamental varieties such as the purple leaved *S. officinalis purpurascens*, although I have found this to be slightly less hardy. 'Tricolor' is variegated with shades of purple and white and 'Icterina' is variegated shades of green and gold. All have lovely aromatic leaves for use in cooking and are also apparently great for cleaning your teeth.

Propagation. Sage grows easily from seed or from semi-ripe cuttings, ideally with a heel, 5-10cm long, in late summer. Pot up rooted cutting into a 1 or 2L pot then plant out once roots start to appear from the holes at the base of the pot.

Maintenance. Check other plants are not smothering it; cut back surrounding foliage if necessary. They are not hungry plants so a layer of organic mulch will be sufficient in autumn, checking the stems are kept clear of mulch to prevent rotting.

Blackcurrants (*Ribes nigrum*)

Blackcurrants are one of my staple crops. I use them in jams, jellies, puddings and fruit leathers. I can't imagine a forest garden without them. They are very easy to grow; the only feeding I do is to mulch each year in autumn but I do occasionally give them a top-up mulch of chopped nettles or comfrey in summer. They will grow happily in full sun or semi-shade. Having said that, I have got one which only gets about an hour's sun a day in mid-summer and is squashed under an *Elaeagnus* and it still fruits. In general the sunnier the spot, the higher your potential yields and the sweeter the fruit. I love the smell of the leaves when harvesting. Once the shrubs are mature, I prune out the oldest one third of branches right back to the ground as I am harvesting. This makes harvesting easier and means I don't need to return to the task later in the year. I have also found that leaving other plants to grow up around the currants, especially nettles or the net forming goosegrass, *Galium aparine*, reduces the amount of crop I lose to birds. I simply cut back surrounding growth at harvest time and throw it under the plant to rot down and feed the blackcurrant.

Choose an upright variety as they create dense shade underneath. 'Ben Hope' is probably the most commonly grown as it is resistant to most pests and diseases and is such a sturdy plant that if attacked, it will probably outgrow any damage. It can get quite large at 2m so not ideal for the smallest gardens although with careful pruning it could be kept smaller. 'Foxendown' is a relatively recent introduction with a lovely upright habit, ideal for small spaces. It has really good disease resistance which is great in an organic system. It fruits early so can be paired with 'Ben Tirran' which fruits in early August to provide a long season of fruit.

Propagation. Blackcurrants can be grown from seed but it is best to grow from cuttings to ensure you get a good cultivated variety. Hardwood cuttings can be taken in winter and are very easy to root; you can put them in pots or a propagation bed but I often strike them directly where I want them to grow in the garden. I have grown a few from seed out of curiosity to see what I might end up with but many suffered from mildew or the fruit size was very disappointing. In a small garden you are better getting a known variety bred for vigour, disease resistance, flavour and yield.

Red, white and pink currants (*Ribes rubrum*)

I use these currants less often than the blackcurrants but they are excellent for jellies and thrive in the shadier spots, although yields will be higher with some sun. The berries are beautifully transparent and look like strings of jewels hanging from the branches. They can be wall-trained where space is limited so can make a feature on a shady wall. My favourite varieties are 'White Versaille', 'Rovada' and 'Pink Champagne' but there are many other varieties out there depending on the size of shrub and what time of year you would like the fruit to ripen.

Propagation. Same as blackcurrants, however pruning is different.

Blackcurrants still ripening in the forest garden

Maintenance. In winter prune out any dead, diseased or dying wood and take out any really old wood which will start to be unproductive. In summer, prune the current year's growth back to two buds to keep the bush to a manageable size. I have to admit to rarely pruning mine so if you prefer a hands-off approach, that's fine. Just be prepared to lose a season's fruit if it gets out of hand one year and you need to do some drastic pruning.

Gooseberry (*Ribes uva-crispa*)

I am not a fan of gooseberries on their own but they are a valuable addition to our fruit leathers and mixed with elderflowers make a heavenly jam. We used to grow them in a fruit cage but they were defoliated every year by the gooseberry sawfly. Now we grow them in the forest garden and the birds pick off the sawfly before they become a problem. I grow 'Invicta' in our forest garden and it has stayed relatively

This gooseberry grows happily and fruits well surrounded by nettles until harvest time

Fruits of *Elaeagnus umbellata* are small and often stolen by the birds before I get to them

compact at just over 1m tall and 1.5m wide with no pruning at all, and fruits very well each year. The accepted way to prune is to achieve a 'goblet' shaped plant to allow air circulation and maximum yields. Cut the current year's growth back by half each year to divert energy to the fruit and remove any inward growing shoots. If you have the time and inclination this will likely produce the maximum amount of fruit in the smallest amount of space but I enjoy a more relaxed approach to fruit growing.

Propagation. Gooseberries are best grown from hardwood cuttings from the previous season's growth. They root very easily.

Maintenance. Pruning as above. I tend to cut back plants around the gooseberry at harvest time and use this as a fresh mulch. If you don't want to trash the surrounding beds and can harvest without damaging the surrounding plants then mulch in autumn.

Elaeagnus umbellata, *E. angustifolia*, *E. multiflora* and *E. x ebbingei*

These are all nitrogen fixing plants with the additional bonus of edible fruit. The fruit flavour and quality varies depending on the species and cultivar and needs to be fully ripe for the best flavour. It can be eaten raw or cooked as a jam. Autumn olive (*E. umbellata*) is my favourite as I just love how the tree looks when it is just coming into leaf, like it's made of silver. Reaching 4.5m at maturity, it can grow to be a very large shrub but can be cut back to keep it at a manageable size; the prunings can then be chopped up and put in the compost or put directly on the ground as a mulch. The flowers have a lovely scent and are very popular with pollinating insects, providing an additional yield of bee forage. Fruits are quite small and it can be a struggle to get to them before the birds but they have so many functions that even if you lose the fruit, you still have the benefits of the additional nitrogen and bee forage. It is happy to grow in poor soils, on exposed sites and in drought conditions making it a valuable shrub for difficult sites.

Propagation. Seed is best sown fresh in a seed bed as stored seed can be slow to germinate. It should germinate by the spring but may remain dormant until the following spring. Seedlings can be transplanted once they are big enough to handle, either into a nursery bed or into pots, until big enough to plant out. They can also be grown from semi-ripe cuttings in summer or hardwood cuttings in late autumn/winter.

Maintenance. None required unless it is getting too big for its allotted space, then either trim with shears or cut whole branches back to the trunk, depending on the look you are going for. As usual, mulch keeps weeds down and moisture in but, as with most nitrogen fixing plants, don't use a nutrient rich mulch; avoid homemade compost and go with rotted leaves.

Sea buckthorn (*Hippophae rhamnoides*)

The flavour of the sea buckthorn fruit is hard to describe but it makes me think of sherbet as it is quite acidic. It is high in vitamin C along with other vitamins and nutrients and can be eaten raw, added to smoothies to give them a bit of a kick or added to fruit leathers. Thanks to its association with a bacteria in the soil, they fix nitrogen so are great to add nutrients to your forest garden. They are happy on poor soils and in exposed situations so great as a productive windbreak, but they can sucker so you will need to keep an eye out and remove any that are growing where you don't want them. They like full sun and will not grow well in shade.

There are male and female plants so make sure you have a male (to pollinate) and a female (to bear the fruit) to ensure you get fruit. Being wind pollinated, make sure they are close to each other to ensure the pollen from the male plant reaches the

Sea buckthorn in autumn as the berries are ripening

Bright orange sea buckthorn berries persist on the branches all winter

female flowers. The bright orange fruit look amazing in the autumn and winter garden and last ages on the branches so you don't need to be in a hurry to harvest them. They can be tricky to harvest as they are quite soft when ripe and can easily crush, not to mention the big thorns on some varieties. One technique to get round this is to use a fork to pull off the fruits whilst holding a bowl underneath. Another more bizarre harvesting technique I have heard of is to prune one third of the fruiting branches at harvest time (this renewal pruning will be discussed below), put the whole fruiting part of the branch in a freezer and once frozen, the berries can be shaken off the branches. I haven't tried this myself but I'm guessing you would need quite a big freezer with lots of room for this method.

Propagation. They can be grown from seed. Seed can be sown in a cold frame and pricked out into pots once big enough to handle. You will then have to distinguish the males from the females. The male seedlings have prominent axillary buds (in the junction between the leaf and the stem) in spring. It is possible to take root cuttings, semi-ripe or hardwood cuttings but the easiest method is to dig up suckers from around the plant and either pot up or plant in their final location.

Maintenance. Pruning keeps bushes at the desired size and keeps them fruiting well. You are best doing a few larger cuts, rather than trimming it a bit with lots of little cuts, as they often don't respond well to trimming like a hedge. Bigger cuts prevent dense growth which makes harvesting more difficult and shades the fruit at the centre of the shrub. They respond well to coppicing so you could cut the whole plant to the ground if it gets too big. A replacement pruning method is best, taking out one third of the oldest fruiting branches each year right down to the base, or back to the main trunk, anytime from late autumn until early spring whilst the plant is dormant. New branches will be encouraged to grow which will be the fruiting wood in the future. Remove any dead, diseased or dying branches at the same time, although it is often easier to spot these in summer when leaves are on the shrub.

Raspberries (*Rubus idaeus*)

Raspberries are such a useful crop to grow at home as they are hard to transport when fully ripe. The ones you buy in a supermarket are often a bit unripe and tasteless as the flavour hasn't been able to develop properly. Raspberries have a reputation for spreading like mad, with new canes sprouting up all around the parent plant. A useful trait in a large-scale forest garden but on a smaller scale it can become a nuisance. There are varieties which are suited to smaller gardens. 'Sugana' fruits both on the previous year's canes in summer and then on the new canes in the autumn, getting a double crop. I have managed to get a similar crop with other autumn fruiting varieties; see below in maintenance. 'Joan J' is quite short at 1.5m, has

Galium aparine (common names include cleavers and sticky willy) covering the raspberries keeping the fruit safe from the birds

Maintenance. Traditionally raspberries are grown in rows for ease of providing support, usually consisting of stakes with wires to which the canes are tied. This does not fit with the lovely natural look of a forest garden. If you choose a variety that does need support, you can grow them in groups of five or six canes, arranged in a circle with a diameter of roughly 60cm-1m, and simply tie the canes together at the top once they have reached their full height, like a self-grown obelisk. Simple and much more attractive than stakes and wires. If growing summer fruiting varieties, cut out the old fruited canes and support or tie up the new canes which will bear the fruit the following year. If growing autumn fruiting varieties, cut all canes to the ground as fruit will be on the canes which grow next year. You could try cutting the fruited canes of autumn varieties back to around 50cm. The previous year's canes produce some fruit in summer with the new canes producing fruit in the autumn. Your autumn crop will most likely be reduced with this method but overall the yield should be equal.

Perennial kales (*Brassica oleracea*)

Not to everyone's taste but I cannot imagine a garden without a perennial kale. They are an important crop in the winter when most fresh greens have died down. 'Taunton Deane' is my most favourite variety by far with its beautiful purple midribs and a melt-in-the-mouth texture when steamed. It is lovely and sweet, not bitter at all. I train this big, vigorous kale into a standard bush by staking its main stem, removing the side branches until it reaches a height of about 1.2m. This means you get the crop of kale but the sunlight can get to the ground below it where you can grow many other crops. Using this method, the 'Taunton Deane' kale becomes the lower canopy layer.

Daubenton 'Panache' is a beautiful variegated variety, preferring shade, which produces more tender leaves. I often shred and use the leaves raw in salads and coleslaws. It is very attractive; the white variegation really lightens up a dark shady corner. Beware that it can sprawl quite far, swamping out other plants if it is happy in its situation. When pruning, you can

delicious large fruits and is sturdy enough to not need staking. 'Autumn Bliss' is another that is pretty much self-supporting. 'All Gold' is my favourite yellow variety. My eldest daughter seeks out the yellow raspberries, eating them all before anyone gets a look-in.

Propagation. New canes are bought in bundles in the winter for planting straight out. Plug plants of young rooted cuttings are becoming more popular but may take longer to establish and fruit. You can lift and divide plants of established, non-diseased patches either to separate the mature canes or dig up the suckering shoots.

Kale 'Taunton Deane' trained as a tree

eat the leaves you cut back, or use them to propagate further plants.

Propagation. Perennial kales rarely flower and the seedling plants may not come true, although I have always found seedlings to be quite similar to the parent. It depends what other brassicas (cabbage, kale, sprouts, broccoli) you may have flowering at the same time and whether they have crossed. They are very easy to grow from cuttings. I often cut a piece off and push it straight into the ground. Choose a small side shoot, remove the leaves from the bottom two thirds of the stem making sure you leave the growing tip, make a hole in the ground or compost with a dibber and insert the cutting with about two thirds under the soil level. Check for pests and remove any plants or weeds that are competing for light and water. If grown in a pot, plant out once roots appear out of the bottom holes in the pot.

Maintenance. Keep an eye out for caterpillar and slug damage. Remove by hand if they become a problem. Spraying with water infused with garlic is said to deter butterflies from laying their eggs on the kale leaves and repels slugs. Wasps have been the most successful pest control for us, carrying off the caterpillars before they do too much damage.

Elder (*Sambucus nigra*)

If you are lucky enough to have a plentiful supply of elderflower to forage for nearby then there is less of a case for including it in a small garden. I use elder-flowers in jams, teas and cordials whilst the fruit goes into fruit leathers, wine and gummies to ward off flu, so it is a valuable plant if you have the space. My favourite cultivated variety is 'Black Lace' with its very dark, finely dissected foliage and pink flowers. They will grow in shade but flower and fruit more

Kale is fully hardy but branches can snap if too much snow weighs them down

Sambucus racemosa 'Sutherlands' has beautifully coloured leaves but I have found the flowers to be smaller than other cultivars

profusely in a sunny spot. They are wind tolerant so good for exposed sites and windbreaks. Some of our best foraging sites are on the edge of the moors as they fruit a week or so later at the higher altitude, once the other elderflowers have gone over. Keep in mind that if you harvest all the flowers, you won't have any berries.

The flowers and fruit of American elder, *Sambucus canadensis*, can be used in the same way as *S. nigra* but are not self-fertile, meaning you will need a pollinator plant if fruit is required.

Propagation. You can grow from seed or softwood, semi-ripe or hardwood cuttings.

Maintenance. To keep to a small size it is best to prune out one third of the oldest, largest branches each year rather than trimming the whole plant with shears as you will be removing flowers or fruits. Elder tends to have a lot of dead wood which can be pruned out any time of year; it is easier to spot in the summer when in leaf.

Fruits of the *Mahonia* x *media* 'Charity' ripening

Oregon grape, *Mahonia* x *media* 'Charity'

I had used this attractive evergreen shrub in planting schemes for years before I realised the fruits are edible. *Mahonia* has very spiky, evergreen foliage producing beautiful yellow scented flowers from November to March. It has a very upright habit, supposedly growing up to 4m tall but I have never seen it reach such heights. It responds well to pruning but they are slow growing so can easily be kept small in a forest garden. The berries ripen in summer and are much loved by birds. They must be cooked and make a delicious jam, but take care when harvesting as the leaves are vicious. They are happy in a wide range of conditions, not being fussy about soil pH or type, happy in dense shade or partial sun. There are many other varieties and species of *Mahonia* with edible berries but *M.* x *media* 'Charity' is my favourite being both beautiful and tasty with a gorgeous scent in winter.

Picking *Mahonia* berries to make jam

Propagation. This is a cultivated variety so best propagated from hardwood cuttings. I have experimented by sowing the seed and ended up with a lovely variety of plants, none of which were quite like the parent but were a great addition to an edible hedge.

Maintenance. Little maintenance is necessary as they grow quite slowly. If it gets too big, prune any stems you feel are too big, right back to about 30cm from the ground and they should reshoot. I have only ever lost one plant using this method. You could remove lower branches to lift the crown of the shrub and plant underneath.

Japonicas (*Chaenomeles japonica, Chaenomeles x superba*)

This is one of my favourite fruits. The small shrubs grow to around 1m in height and can be grown up a wall. The spring flowers are beautiful with cultivars available in shades of white, pink and red. They are fantastic for wildlife, attracting many pollinators into the garden early in the year. The fruit are yellow when ripe and very hard, staying on the shrub right into winter. They need to be cooked but are very fragrant raw, especially if you keep a bowlful in the house like a natural potpourri. We add them to fruit leather, jams and jellies but they make a delicious jam just by themselves.

Propagation. Seed can be sown fresh outdoors and will germinate quickly. Seedlings can be planted out the following year. Semi-ripe cuttings can be taken in late summer or hardwood cuttings in winter. Cultivated varieties will need to be grown from cuttings as they won't come true from seed.

Maintenance. They are very easy to grow with little else than a mulch needed. They are quite low-growing shrubs so keep free of tall weeds or competition from other vigorous plants. They can be pruned to manage their size and spread.

Andrew's dad found a japonica bush with very large japonica fruits in a garden near his house and the owner kindly let him pick them

Herbaceous layer

Daylily (Hemerocallis sp.)

There are so many varieties of this lily-like flower to choose from so you should find one to suit your colour scheme (if you have one). There are delicate dwarf varieties and huge vigorous ones, so check their height and spread before buying. You can extend the season of flowers available by choosing both early and late flowering varieties to grow together. Unopened flower pods can be added to stir fries or once opened, tear off the petals to liven up a salad. Every part of the plant, including the roots, is edible but not as delicious as the flowers.

Propagation. They are so easy to grow from divisions. Simply dig up a clump and either slice off chunks with a sharp knife or use two forks back to back to prise the clump apart. Replant these divisions or pot up to give away or swap.

Maintenance. Cut back in winter or spring and either 'chop and drop' leaving the dead plant material in situ or add to the compost heap. The annual mulch over the whole forest garden should be enough to feed the plants. Lift and divide clumps if they start to spread too far.

Onion family (*Allium* sp.)

There are so many fantastic plants in the onion family, it is a must to include at least one or two. Traditional onion sets that are grown in vegetable gardens do not thrive in a polyculture setting unless given a lot of space; they do not like competition at all. This is true of many of the onion family, but not of wild garlic (*Allium ursinum*) which tends to be a thug. Wild garlic is one of my favourite plants for cooking with. I make pesto, salads, fritters and more, but a word of caution is needed. I planted some in a polyculture bed and it has been a nightmare ever since, spreading like mad and killing off other plants. I would recommend you find a patch in the wild to forage from, or plant under some trees or shrubs where you are not growing anything else that is precious.

This daylily is planted with a variegated *Astrantia*, *Rudbeckia* 'Goldsturm', golden marjoram and lavender mint

I often plant garlic cloves or whole bulbs in the ground and treat them as a perennial crop. Each year the green shoots emerge before most other plants have got going. I harvest them as I would chives, sprinkling them on soup or mixing with butter to make garlic bread. Once the chives appear, I switch to using those and let the garlic grow undisturbed for the rest of the year. One patch has been growing beneath a trained pear for nearly a decade, smothered by *Physalis* later in the year, but never fails to pop back up in spring.

Chives are very easy to grow and can be harvested for a very long period throughout the spring, summer and autumn. I like to grow three clumps at least: one to be harvesting whilst the other two grow, then I cut the clump right down and switch to harvesting the next one. The third patch is allowed to flower as I love to

Garlic chive flower sitting high above the surrounding groundcover plants

The head of bulbils from perennial Babington leek. I will break this head apart and pot up the bulbils.

sprinkle the flowers on pizza and in salads. By the time the third clump is looking a bit tired, I cut it right to the ground and start using clump number one again. This intensive way of managing the plants means they enjoy a boost from some liquid feed a few times a year.

Garlic chives are a very pretty addition to the forest garden. Their flowers are held high above the soil on rigid stems, making them ideal in a polyculture as they don't flop over and squash other plants. I mostly use the flowers but the leaves can also be eaten.

Perennial leeks
(*Allium ampeloprasum*)

Allium ampeloprasum var. 'Babingtonii' is a native wild leek and an ancestor of our cultivated leek. It emerges in winter/spring and is harvested between March and June; it then becomes dormant and dies down. For this reason it is ideal for the back of a border so other plants can grow up in front of it and hide the dead stems. When harvesting, cut back to the base of the stem but don't dig up the bulbs as these will grow again next year. Ideally, harvest half of

the stems, not all, so the plant has enough energy to grow back next year. Stems allowed to grow will also bear bulbils where you would expect flowers to be; these bulbils can be planted to grow on.

This is just a selection of the alliums I use the most but there are many more such as Hooker's onion (*Allium acuminatum*), Welsh onion (*Allium fistulosum*) and walking onion (*Allium* x *proliferum*).

Propagation. They can all be propagated by division. Some have obvious bulbs such as wild garlic, others have more matted roots such as chives. I have found the best time of year for this is when the plant is just coming into growth; this avoids rotting. Some alliums produce bulbils on their flower heads which can be separated and planted straight out or potted up to grow on.

Maintenance. A cut back and annual mulch is all that is required. Chives can often get rust and look unappetising. Cut them right to the ground and water with organic liquid feed. They should grow back quickly and look lush and green.

Hooker's onion tumbling onto the paving at the edge of the bed

Golden marjoram (bottom edge of photo) goes well with
the zesty yellow/green of the *Smyrnium perfoliatum*

Golden marjoram (*Origanum vulgare* 'Aurea')

It is a form of wild marjoram with golden leaves. In my yard where sunlight is more limited, the leaves are more of a lime green. It is a fantastic zesty contrast to the other green foliage plants in the edible borders. It is a woody perennial growing to just 30cm but sprawling outwards. I use it on the edge of borders where it thrives without competition from taller plants. I snip pieces off to use in soups, stews and sparingly in salads. Bunches can be gathered in summer and hung to dry for use through the winter. Alongside chives, this is probably the most used plant in my yard forest garden. It looks stunning in spring when the zingy lime-green flowers of *Smyrnium perfoliatum* are blooming above it, contrasting with the blue spires of *Camassia leichtlinii*.

Propagation. Other oreganos can be grown from seed but 'Aurea' is a cultivated variety so needs to be propagated by cuttings or division. You can take tip cuttings in summer but I find the easiest method is to find a section along the stem where it has been in contact with the ground and started to develop roots. Cut the stem from the plant, find the section with roots and trim back the stem either side of this, then pot up and grow on until large enough to plant out. You can pin the stem to the ground with a piece of bent wire to hold it in place until roots develop. I have tried digging the whole plant up to divide but the crown is so woody it tends to snap and tear then rot.

Maintenance. Other than harvesting, the only maintenance required is a cut back in the winter and a mulch, taking care to leave the crown of the plant clear of mulch or it can encourage rotting.

Lupins (*Lupinus* sp.)

I grew lupins in my first ever patch of garden I was given at the age of seven or eight. I grew to think of them as a bit twee, that was until I discovered they fix nitrogen. They fit beautifully into edible polycultures as an annual to fill gaps and provide nutrients. They are prone to slug damage so I like plants to be quite large before I plant them out, then keep a close eye on them until they are big enough to fend for themselves. Most lupins have toxic seeds containing high levels of alkaloids, requiring a lot of soaking and processing to become edible, however there are edible varieties specifically bred for human consumption. Edible lupins have a higher quality of protein than soya and, unlike soya, are suited to our climate. The white lupin, *Lupinus albus*, is more suited to warmer, drier regions of the UK. A white variety called 'Dieta' was bred in the UK and grows to a height of around 60cm-1m. The blue lupin, *Lupinus angustifolius*, of which 'Haags Blue' is a variety, is more suited to the cooler wetter regions of the UK, growing to a height of around 50-70cm. I have yet to try these edible lupins but they are top of my list for trying out next growing season. It would be great to give the lupin the added function of edibility alongside fixing nitrogen, looking beautiful and as a pollinator attractor.

Lupinus arboreus, the tree lupin, can be damaged by frost so we have planted it against a wall to reduce the risk of frost damage

Propagation. There are both hardy perennial and half hardy annual lupins. Edible lupins are an annual; sow seeds each spring around April and plant out once they are above 10cm tall. Allow some seed to mature on the plant and save to resow the following year. Ensure there are no other lupins growing nearby as they will cross readily and you could end up saving toxic seed.

Maintenance. Keep the slugs off while the plants are still young and vulnerable. Keep watered in dry weather and stake if they are blowing over and starting to smother out other crops. Aphids can sometimes be a problem, especially in dry weather. Leave the aphids for as long as you can to attract beneficial insects to deal with the problem. If they continue to be a problem, spray with a soap solution or preferably, cut the flower stem and remove to the compost heap where you won't have to look at them but the ladybirds can still feast upon them.

Mint (*Mentha*)

There are many, many mints to choose from depending on what you are using it for. The two I can't do without are:

Spearmint or garden mint: *Mentha spicata*. I use this in cooking, especially for making crab apple and mint jelly. If I had room for just one mint it would be this one. I try to cut some and keep it in the kitchen in a glass of water so it's close at hand when cooking; it stays fresh all week.

Peppermint: *Mentha* x *piperita*. I especially love the variety 'Swiss' as a mint tea. Whenever I serve a mug full to friends, I always get compliments. It has a lovely minty, fresh but sweet flavour.

Lavender mint is third on my list as actual lavender doesn't grow well in my yard but this lovely delicate mint thrives there. It has attractive purplish stems and leaves and is less of a thug than most mints. I like to run the stems through my hands whilst doing my forest garden observations, and breathe in the minty, lavender scent. I use a steam extractor to harvest the

Mint growing underneath a fruit tree alongside some oregano in the 'Veg on the Edge' community forest garden in Saltaire, Yorkshire

juice to use in homemade soap and shampoo bars.

Propagation. It is very easy to grow from cuttings. Simply cut off the top 10cm of a non-flowering stem, remove the bottom leaves and sit in a glass of water until roots begin to appear, then pot up in multi-purpose compost and plant out once a good root system has developed. Another easy method is to cut off a rhizome and pin it down in a seed tray full of compost until rooted, or bury a section of rhizome just under the soil, directly in the forest garden.

Maintenance. It can spread like crazy so surround the plant with a barrier of some kind, ideally a sunken pot with the bottom removed, or the rim of a pot. I have also used slates half buried to make a box around the plant. This prevents the plants from sending out runners across the soil and taking over the whole bed. I have found runners growing 1m long in one season.

Ground covers

Strawberry and wild/alpine strawberry (*Fragaria* ssp.)

My preference for ground cover in a forest garden is usually to use the wild or alpine strawberry over the more cultivated garden strawberry *Fragaria* x *ananassa*. The main considerations are that the garden strawberry has been bred to grow in ideal conditions with no competition; it is prone to more diseases and they tend to fruit over a much shorter period of time.

There is much debate over the difference between alpine and wild strawberries but they are now both classified as *Fragaria vesca*. The main difference is that wild strawberries tend to spread by runners and alpine ones are more clump forming. Both have their place. Spreading by runners means the strawberry can spread about underneath other plants, find a place it likes and smother out the plants

we don't want. If we plant them along the front of a border or along a path, the runners can become a bit of a nuisance, and a trip hazard, so in that situation you may choose the clumping form. I have grown both and still tend to use those that spread by runners because they are easy to propagate vegetatively. Clumping forms tend to produce more fruit but can be so productive that they burn out after two or three years and need replacing which is more work than I like in a system that should be relatively self-sustaining.

There is a good selection of varieties available and all fruits should be left to be fully ripe to develop their wonderful fragrant flavour. I have a yellow/white form *Fragaria* 'Pineapple Crush' which I was given and is much less sought after by the birds than the red ones as they are fooled into thinking they are

The wild strawberry can be used as ground cover and planted in pallet planters or green walls

Yellow varieties fool the birds into leaving them alone; they are often still fruiting right into winter

not yet ripe. The birds are really missing out as they are delicious with a hint of pineapple. You can't tell ripeness by colour as they stay pale yellow, but they become much softer when ripe, much softer than a garden strawberry. We taught the kids to do a simple delicate squeeze test when they were little to ensure they didn't pick them all too soon. 'White Soul' is a beautiful little white variety, 'Mignonette' is probably the most commonly grown red alpine strawberry which is popular as it doesn't produce runners so is easy to keep under control, not necessarily a good quality if you want a rampant ground cover, but great for more controlled situations such as around herbs and other small plants. In my experience they grow well in both sun and semi-shade but need at least three or four hours of sun a day to fruit well.

Propagation. Most clumping varieties spread to around 30 x 30cm, those with runners are almost infinite but, with their shallow roots, are easily pulled up in areas you don't want them. If propagating from runners, pin down the little plantlets to the soil or into a pot placed in the garden in situ next to the parent plant. Roots form easily and they can be detached or transplanted once they have rooted. They grow easily from seed if you are careful with the watering. Sow the seed in a tray or pot then place this into a tray of water to soak up from below. The seed is very fine and can easily be washed to the edges or too deep into the soil to germinate. Seed should germinate within a few weeks. Spring-sown seed can be producing fruit by the autumn so it is worth considering this method if you require a large number of plants. They often self-seed in the garden so it is worth keeping an eye out and save yourself the bother of germinating the seed. Carefully dig up and pot up the tiny seedlings and grow on until big enough to plant out elsewhere or to replace the parent plants if they are losing vigour.

Maintenance. They are woodland plants and thrive if given a good mulch each year. A sprinkling of wood ash can help increase fruiting. I have heard they love a mulch of pine needles but haven't tried this myself. Clumping varieties will need replacing every few years as they lose vigour. Runners may need cutting back in areas where you need a bit more control.

Viola sororia 'Freckles'

This is such a pretty groundcover plant. I love to use it at the front of borders as it is quite a compact plant at around 25-30cm in height. It spreads around and clumps up nicely, filling any gaps with very dense growth, preventing any weed seeds from finding somewhere to germinate. The flowers are the star of the plant, so pretty and delicate enough to sit atop the daintiest of cupcakes. They make the most boring of salads look beautiful. The leaves and flower buds can also be added to salads in moderation; the young leaves are more tender and have a nicer flavour. There are many varieties but 'Freckles' is my favourite. All viola have edible flowers so you have the option of winter flowering varieties to liven up your winter dishes.

Propagation. They are easy to grow from seed but if you want a specific variety it is best to grow from divisions. Dig up a clump anytime between autumn and early spring and simply pull off sections for replanting elsewhere or to pot up. You can divide *Viola sororia* into quite small sections if you are wanting lots of plants to cover a large area; they are best potted up if you are doing this to allow them to grow into decent sized plants before planting out.

Maintenance. A simple mulch and cut back are all that is required. They are very low maintenance.

Viola sororia 'Freckles' is a highly effective groundcover plant producing flowers over a long period in spring/summer

Symphytum ibericum covering the ground under some silver birch, thriving despite the very dry soil conditions

Campanula growing out of a crack in a garden wall

Creeping comfrey (*Symphytum* sp.)

There are several varieties of low-growing, creeping comfrey such as *S. grandiflorum* and *S. ibericum* growing to just 30cm. My favourite is *Symphytum* 'Hidcote Blue' with its delicate floral croziers starting as red, then unfurling to shades of white and blue, flowering from February right into May. I have seen it successfully growing in both deep shade and full sun and on all soil types. Beware, it can take over if paired with other delicate plants so is best used under hedges and in difficult places where other plants would struggle to grow, rather than in the middle of a polyculture bed.

Propagation. It can be lifted and divided very easily. Cut all foliage back when dividing to reduce water stress on the plant until it has formed roots.

Maintenance. I just leave it to it. It stays semi-evergreen in mild winters. If I want to make comfrey feed then I just give it a good trim with shears to harvest the leaves; it quickly recovers.

Campanula (*C. portenschlagiana* and *C. porcharskyana*)

These species have a profusion of pretty purple edible flowers, spreading like a mat across the soil. They are a very effective ground cover, especially suited to rockery situations or in walls. The leaves are also edible but the texture can be a bit dry so use sparingly with other greens. It is semi-evergreen so leaves are often available all winter. I have used these in a green wall as they seem just as happy spreading upwards and trailing down as they are spreading outwards.

Propagation. By seed in a tray of seed compost, can be sown outside and pricked out when seedlings are large enough to handle. They are very easy to divide and a small clump can be split into many tiny pieces and potted up.

Maintenance. Mulch in autumn but otherwise no maintenance is required unless you want to tidy away dead stems in autumn.

Rhizome layer

Chinese artichoke (*Stachys affinis*)

This plant produces a small tuber which, although quite tasty eaten raw or cooked, is pretty fiddly to clean and process. The flower is very pretty so it adds colour and food for pollinators along with an edible tuber. The tubers start to swell later in the year so don't be in a hurry to dig them up; October is usually a good time to dig your first harvest. Chinese artichoke are happy in most soils and are fairly easy to grow. The leaves die down over winter but the tubers can be left in the ground until you want to eat them, otherwise they can dry out in storage.

Propagation. A few tubers are simply replanted each year. In all honesty it's almost impossible to find every single tuber even if you are trying. The few that get left behind begin to grow in the spring. Tubers can be planted into compost in pots in early spring if you want some to give away. Otherwise they are much happier planted directly in the ground in your desired location.

Maintenance. I have never had problems with pests or diseases. Simply cut back when you decide they look too messy and harvest between October and February/March. The usual annual mulch is all the feeding they require unless they start to look hungry (if the leaves look pale or the plants look stunted), then they could benefit from a liquid feed boost or additional mulch.

Jerusalem artichokes (*Helianthus tuberosus*)

Related to sunflowers, these perennial plants have edible tubers with a reputation for giving you wind. Cooking with winter savory is meant to aid digestion and reduce flatulence. You can get a substantial amount of tubers from each plant so they are well worth growing; some varieties have quite large tubers so they are much easier to process than the Chinese artichoke. The plant is very tall at about 2m so they

The tiny tubers of the Chinese artichoke are small and fiddly to clean but very easy to grow with a very pretty flower

are best for the back of a border where they will give a beautiful sunny display of yellow flowers at the end of summer. Harvest in autumn as the plant starts to die back and turn brown. To keep the patch perennial, simply leave some of the tubers in the ground.

Propagation. They produce tubers that can be planted back into the ground or into pots with multi-purpose compost. They are not very happy in small pots as the plants are quite large so plant out as soon as you can.

Maintenance. Other than harvesting, there is little to do other than to cut back in the autumn and mulch. They are very easy plants to grow.

Oca (*Oxalis tuberosa*)

Like little shiny jewels dug from the soil, oca comes in a range of colours from pale yellow to red and pink. Cultivated for thousands of years in South America, they are very commonly eaten in New Zealand and becoming increasingly popular in the UK. They are a bit hardier than potatoes with the added benefit of being fairly pest and disease-free. The tubers are quite small but tasty. They can be eaten raw when they have a fresh lemony flavour, or baked as you would a potato. The tubers develop late in the season so don't be in a hurry to dig them up. The foliage is often killed off by frost but the tubers are protected underground and I have quite a few patches of perennial oca, even in my cold northern garden. The foliage and flowers are a very pretty addition to any garden but can spread quite far, around 40-60cm, so give them plenty of room.

Propagation. The tubers can be planted direct or potted up and kept in an unheated greenhouse if you are feeling cautious.

Maintenance. Cut back, if you want to tidy up, once the frosts have killed off the foliage and apply a mulch. A deep mulch will help to protect the tubers from any penetrating ground frosts. I have never had any issues with pests or diseases.

Oca being prepared in the kitchen, ready for a stir fry

Earthnut pea

Earthnut pea (*Lathyrus tuberosus*)

This is a very pretty short climber with bright pink, scented flowers grown for its edible leaves and tubers. It is herbaceous so dies down each year, its stems growing to around 1.2m either up a support, another nearby plant or trailing along the ground. It has the added benefit of fixing nitrogen, giving added nutrition to plants growing nearby. The tubers can be eaten raw but tend to be bland in flavour. Once cooked the tubers have a delicious nutty flavour. The main reason this plant has never become a staple crop is that yields are low, but I feel it's worth growing due to the added benefits of the beautiful flowers and the added nutrition it brings to the soil. It will grow in a wide range of soils, especially poor soils deficient in nitrogen and even tolerating high soil salinity.

Propagation. They are not easy from seed as germination rates tend to be low so best to grow from the tubers. Dig up plants, divide the tubers then plant out or pot up to grow on.

Maintenance. You could provide support such as an obelisk around 1.5m high for the plant to climb, or plant near a shrub or small tree that won't mind the competition, such as a blackcurrant. Cut back once the foliage has turned brown and mulch. It prefers a poorer soil, as do many nitrogen fixers, so don't liquid feed with a high nitrogen feed.

Quamash (*Camassia quamash*, also *C. leichtlinii*)

This is one of my most favourite bulbs, though I have never eaten it because it is so beautiful – I can't quite bring myself to dig it up. The baked bulb was a staple food of the Native Americans and can be used in place of potatoes. It is said to have a chestnutty flavour. I love this plant in my forest garden because it pushes its way through other perennials in spring, taking up almost no space on the ground, producing beautiful deep blue spires of star-like flowers. Even if, like me, you can't quite bring yourself to eat it, it is still a wonderful addition to any polyculture.

Propagation. You can grow this from seed but it will take a few years for the seedlings to produce a bulb large enough to flower. The bulbs are not expensive so it's easier and still economical to buy as bulbs and plant direct in autumn.

Maintenance. Very easy; just leave them alone, cutting back dead stems if you want to tidy up. If you want to harvest some, they will need a few years to bulk up. Once harvested, replant a few bulbs to bulk up again.

Camassia leichtlinii growing in the yard forest garden

Climbers

Hardy kiwi (*Actinidia arguta*)

The fruits are much smaller than the common kiwi you would recognise in the shops, about the size of a large grape. They grow pretty big, up to 6m, so require a large surface to be trained up, not one for really small gardens, however they can be pruned to keep in check. They can take many years to produce fruit and you need both a male and female plant for pollination to happen to ensure you get fruit on the female plants. They like free draining, acidic soils and are not as hardy as their name would suggest, so not ideal for all gardens but one I wanted to include as climbers are handy for an added yield if you have the vertical space to train them up.

Propagation. Cuttings can be tricky to root but I always like to give it a try before purchasing a plant. Cuttings, of current season's growth with a diameter of around 1cm, can be taken at the end of summer, ideally three nodes long, cutting it from the vine just below a node, and taking off the growing tip just above a node. Place the cutting in a pot with a free draining mix of compost and perlite and keep the humidity levels up by placing a plastic bag over the pot to form a sort of mini greenhouse, or keep in a propagator, and mist several times a day, keeping at around 20°C. After a few weeks, roots should have started to form. After six weeks, cuttings should be ready to transplant to a bigger pot to grow on. Grow in an unheated greenhouse or cold frame for the first year until the plant is large enough to withstand frosts.

Maintenance. Winter pruning helps to create a good branch structure whilst summer pruning helps to keep the plant to size and reduce vigour. The hardy kiwi fruits on the current season's wood which comes from one-year-old wood. Older fruited wood is much less productive so can be removed to give way for younger fruiting shoots. During summer cut back new stems 4-6 leaves from the last flowers; this helps to reduce vigour and divert energy to fruit development. Remove watersprouts (vigorous shoots coming from the trunk) and other stems that are swamping other plants. A mulch is all that is required for feeding.

Caucasian spinach (*Hablitzia tamnoides*)

I love spinach but the annual plant can be hard to grow, bolting easily and needing sowing each year from seed. This climber comes back each year, has edible spinach-like leaves which can be harvested over a long period and has the added bonus of being a climber so it takes up very little ground space in the forest garden. They prefer semi-shade which is very helpful as so many edible plants require lots of sun. They can grow up to 3m so need a good framework or a sturdy tree. You can harvest and eat the shoot tips to keep them to a smaller size if needed. There are not many perennial 'greens' that I think are tasty enough to warrant growing so this plant is a valuable addition to the forest garden.

Propagation. They can be grown easily from seed. Simply sow in a seed tray in autumn/winter and leave in a cold frame or unheated greenhouse to germinate. If sowing in spring the seed will need stratifying in a fridge for 7-10 days in some damp compost, then sown in a seed tray. Once big enough, seedlings should be pricked out into pots and planted out once big enough to compete in the garden, which depends on what you are growing around them. Mature plants can also be lifted and divided.

Maintenance. Plants may need tying in as they grow, depending on the structure they are growing up. Pruning to keep plants to required size can be done at any time of year. Seed can be collected in autumn from plants that flower. You will need a few plants to get good pollination and viable seed. A deep mulch helps to protect the plant over winter.

Berries of the magnolia vine

Magnolia vine or wu wei zi (*Schisandra chinensis*)

This fragrant spring flowering deciduous climber produces small bunches of fruits in the autumn. Plants are either male or female so you will need one of each for pollination. Fruit is sweet and sour, traditionally eaten dried like a raisin and used in Chinese medicine. The young tender leaves can be cooked as greens. It can grow to over 8m but can be pruned to keep to size. It is not fussy about soil type but does like it moist and free draining. *Schisandra* is not happy in full sun so plant in shade or semi-shade, even up a north facing wall, although young shoots can be damaged by frost in spring so planting under a tree canopy can provide some protection. It is a pretty climber but something I rarely eat so only include if you have the space and want to try something different.

Propagation. Seed can be sown in autumn in a cold frame or unheated greenhouse although germination from seed can be poor. Semi-ripe cuttings can be taken in late summer. Young cuttings or seedlings should be kept in a shaded position in the greenhouse or cold frame as they dislike full sun.

Maintenance. Dead or dying wood can be removed in winter or spring. If shoots are taking over where they are not wanted, they can be cut back at any time although the plant is fairly slow growing. Shoots need tying in periodically. A good mulch should provide enough nutrients, especially if planted with nutrient accumulators.

This is just a small selection of the plants you could include in your forest garden; there are so many amazing plants I could fill a whole other book. My advice is to visit as many forest gardens as you can, and try to taste as many plants as you can before committing to growing them. If something is not working, don't be afraid to remove and replace it. My biggest mistake when getting started was assuming everything had to be edible or it wasn't a real forest garden. I now embrace the many functions of the non-edible plants, giving food to wildlife and much joy to myself, family and friends. Experiment, observe and interact, and enjoy the journey of becoming a forest gardener.

The polyculture bed outside the eco meeting
room at Ecology Building Society H.Q. in Silsden

Going Forward